Swimming Against the Tide

Swimming Against the Tide

A retelling of the story of Joni Eareckson Tada – Some conversations and situations have been altered or combined with permission

Catherine Mackenzie

Christian Focus Publications

Copyright © 2003 Catherine Mackenzie
ISBN 1-85792-833-4

Published by Christian Focus Publications,
Geanies House, Fearn, Tain, Ross-shire, IV20 1TW, Scotland,
United Kingdom.
www.christianfocus.com
email: info@christianfocus.com

Thinking further topics and suplementary details
including time line provided by the author.

Cover design by Alister Macinnes.
Cover illustration by Neil Reed.
Printed and bound in Great Britain by
Cox and Wyman, Reading, United Kingdom.

All rights reserved. No part of this publication may be reproduced,
stored in a retrieval system, or transmitted, in any form, by any
means, electronic, mechanical, photocopying, recording or otherwise
without the prior permission of the publisher or a license permitting
restricted copying. In the U.K. such licenses are issued by the
Copyright Licensing Agency, 90 Tottenham Court Road, London
W1P 9HE.

Joni Eareckson Tada: Life Summary adapted from the Joni and Friends
website www.joniandfriends.org
The quote from President Bush is also available for review on the
same website.

Contents

On April 10th, 2002
during a meeting at
the White House,
President George W. Bush commented
to Joni Eareckson Tada,
'I want to thank you for
your courage;
I want to thank you for
your wisdom;
I want to thank you for
your extraordinary perseverance and faith.
You have triumphed in the face of
physical disability.'

Joni, it has been an immense privilege to write this book — a retelling of your life — or at least parts of it. God has given me, and others, the opportunity to see His grace and power through your days and nights, tears and laughter, fears and hopes. It is no mean feat to open your life to scrutiny in the way you have done through book and film. I have been humbled, encouraged, taught and inspired by your story and by the power and intimacy of The One True God whom we both call Father.

With love and thanks,
Catherine Mackenzie

Life Choices?

'Oh I don't know, I can't even choose what cereal to eat in the morning – how do they expect me to know whether I should take a for algebra, b for biology or c for cookery?' James' scowl said it all – he was a bit annoyed, but mostly bored and he certainly couldn't be bothered to look at next year's subject choices.

'Well, for starters,' Jenny piped up, 'they don't call it cookery. It's domestic science – and please don't take it James because I've eaten your cheese on toast – pleasant it wasn't.' She flicked her long blonde hair across one shoulder before leaning over to study the subject list their teacher had just given them yesterday morning. Saturday was usually spent down at the park or browsing through the CDs on the market... but today was different. Jenny and James had to decide about next year's time table.

'If I choose biology in this column,' Jenny continued, 'I won't be able to take languages... and then there's drama and I love drama.'

Jenny sighed and reached out to the fruit bowl for a juicy red apple. Choosing subjects for next year was going to be tricky. The screen door slammed and soon Garry was in the kitchen with them. Garry, James and Jenny had been friends since nursery and kindergarten and they had decided that three heads were much better than one when making major life changing decisions – and it would be more fun anyway!

Garry's hair was damp from his swimming practice. A strong smell of mint filled the air as he stood there, relaxed, chewing gum.

Jenny sighed again. 'Are either of you taking this seriously? James is chattering on about taking cookery – all you can think of is swimming. I mean if I take languages and not drama then I might never be an actress! And I'm good at drama – my teacher says so.'

'Yeah, yeah,' James rolled his eyes to the ceiling. 'Good at drama. Well, Jenny, you'd have to be – you're such a drama queen!'

Garry chuckled, 'People say that you shouldn't "Make a drama out of a crisis," – well you can't help yourself. So go ahead, Jenny, ditch languages, your audience awaits you.' And with that Garry swept the floor with a large theatrical bow.

Jenny gave both boys a long steely stare. 'Some friends you are! This is important. Don't you know it affects all our futures?'

James lifted his eyes to the ceiling once more. 'I know, I know. But come on you're taking things too seriously. Lighten up. I know we should think about what we're going to do with our lives but we're just getting a bit too stressed about all this subjects and choices and future stuff.'

'Too serious? Lighten up? Too Stressed?' With each word Jenny's voice seemed to raise an octave.

'If you make a wrong choice now it could muck things up big time! And that would be serious. Much too serious!'

James looked at Jenny's flushed cheeks and leant back in his chair.

'O.K. then, so we should be thinking more about our futures... perhaps it would help us all to do just that.' In a very serious tone James turned to Jenny and exclaimed, 'What do you want to do with your life?'

'Oh, don't make fun of it, James!'

'I'm not, seriously. What do you want to do?'

'Well,' Jenny thought a little, 'I suppose I am good at drama. I might get a job acting or on TV or something... It's not totally silly!' Jenny finished off loudly as a smirk began to spread across Garry's face. 'If you think it's that funny,' Jenny continued, 'Tell us what you want to be!'

Garry was stumped for a little and then he blushed. 'Well, I was thinking about becoming a doctor.'

Jenny snorted. 'You'll have to work hard then. Your grades will need to improve for a start!'

'I know,' Garry sighed. 'But I think I can do it if I really try. I just hope I can keep up the swimming with all the extra study that I'll have to do.'

James nodded. 'Too right. You're the best swimmer on the team. But I suppose it's like the careers guy said we all have to make choices.'

'And some of us will have to make changes,' Jenny said in a rather superior tone.

Both boys ignored her and carried on their conversation, 'I want to be a doctor because I want to do something that will really make a difference to people's lives. I'd be learning to heal people. What about you, James – what do you want to do?'

Jenny turned round in her seat, curious about what her friend was going to say. 'Do you even know what you want to do?' she asked.

'Sure I do,' James smiled. 'I'm going to rock everyone's world with my guitar. So long as I'm taking music I don't care what other subjects I do. But I suppose I'd better take English so that I can write my memoirs afterwards!'

Garry laughed out loud and it was Jenny's turn to raise her eyes to the ceiling. 'James, I reckon you should be a comedian – you never take things seriously.'

'No,' Garry giggled, 'With his looks he should be a clown and save stacks of money on the make-up.'

That comment promptly started a tea-towel fight in the middle of the kitchen as the two boys chased each other round the room. Jenny continued to study the subject list, choosing to leave her two best friends to their games.

Just then the door opened and James' mum walked in, grabbing the tea towels and putting them neatly back inside the drawer.

'I see the careers discussion is coming along well,' she said with a smile tweaking at the edges of her mouth. 'Made any decisions yet?'

'No,' was the answer from all three.

'Well, you'll be discussing it with your parents tonight no doubt. James' dad is going to have a chat with him.'

James didn't raise his eyes to the ceiling this time. Instead he blushed and looked at the floor.

Garry sniggered, 'Mrs D. I think it's great that James wants to do Music and English to further his singing career.'

With that Mrs D. burst out laughing. 'Singing career? James? You should have heard him first thing this morning in the shower! James, I think you'd better re-think that one.'

'I never said singing,' James growled, 'I said guitar! I can play quite well you know!'

'That's true,' Mrs D. nodded. 'But there certainly are some difficult choices for you kids this year.'

Jenny interrupted. 'So how do I know if I'm making the right ones?'

'That's a tricky question but the future isn't up to you. Though you have to make choices and do your best it's good to know that the future is in God's control. Ask him to guide you about any choices you have to make... I can give advice... but he'll move you in the right direction if you ask him to.'

Jenny twiddled with a lock of blonde hair and then sighed. 'I suppose we should be thankful that we can make choices. Some people don't have that freedom. Their choices are made for them.'

'Yeah,' James nodded. 'Like Garry wants to be a doctor but he's also a really good swimmer. At least he has the choice. I've never really thought of it like that before.'

Mrs D. sat down beside them all at the kitchen table and brought out a small worn paperback from her handbag. 'I know this woman who was a brilliant swimmer.' She told the others. 'She wasn't much older than you are now but one day she made a choice that changed her life for ever.'

'How come?' Garry asked puzzled.

'Well first things first. This woman was a brilliant swimmer but she is also an artist, a musician, a writer and an actress.'

'Wow, that's amazing,' exclaimed Jenny.

'Yes, and her story all begins on a beautiful summer's day when Joni Eareckson went swimming, dived beneath the water and broke her neck.'

'You're kidding,' Garry gasped. 'What did she do then?'

'She couldn't do much, idiot,' James nudged his pal in the shoulder. 'She was paralysed.'

'Well you're wrong there, James,' Mrs D. continued. 'Joni has set up an organisation to help handicapped people around the world. She runs fund raisers, writes books, she did a film, she sings at concerts, she drives a car, paints pictures... with her mouth... and this is all after she became paralysed and had to live her life in a wheelchair.'

'Gosh,' Jenny muttered stuck for words – for once. 'How did she do it?'

'Well there's only one answer to that question. She faced her challenges with God's help and with God's help her wheelchair became a tool for spreading God's love – instead of a tragedy. It took a lot to bring her to that point, but that's what God did. That day when she dived beneath the waves was the last day that she could swim, run or walk... but it was the first day of the rest of her life... a life that showed God's love to people who needed him... with or without a disability. It's a wonderful story.'

'Yeah,' James gasped. 'I'd love to read a book like that.'

'You read a book?' Mrs D. smiled. 'Well I suppose if you're going to take English next year you'd better get in some practice.' Passing over the paperback she said to James, 'Seeing as I need to get something for lunch you can start reading Joni's story while I get it ready.' But just then Jenny took the book from James and handed it back to his mum.

'No, Mrs D.' Jenny smirked. 'James said earlier how he's keen on doing cookery. You read the book... and perhaps James could stretch to ordering us all a Pizza?'

'Great idea!' said Mrs D., Garry and James.

That Day on the Beach

The 30th of July 1967 was like every other summer's day in Maryland USA. Joni Eareckson was planning a beach party with her friends – the phone perched between her ear and her chin as she frantically organised the last minute details.

'Just a few of us … we'll hang out at Chesapeake Bay. Come if you can. Bring some food… yeah a salad would be great… Butch is bringing the drinks. Yeah… yeah… that's Kathy's new boyfriend. He's not bad … and at least he's got wheels… wait … hang on a sec Kathy's shouting …What do you want, sis?' Joni yelled up the stairs.

'I said… get off the phone. Butch'll be here any minute … or he might be calling me to say he'll be late.You've been on for over an hour. How many are you asking to this thing anyway?'

Joni raised her eyes to the ceiling with a sigh, 'Sorry about that… it's just my older overbearing sister telling me what to do as usual!'

'I heard that!' Kathy yelled down the stairs once more.

Ignoring the slamming bedroom door Joni carried on the telephone conversation. 'We're going to be there oh-probably mid afternoon. We might get a barbecue going. But I just can't wait to hit the water! It's so hot! But talking about hot – I've got the coolest swim suit! Yeah… electric blue, got it yesterday. Dick is bound to love it. But I'd better go – I've got my stuff to pack yet.You know the drill – you never know who you might meet on the beach so look your best.'

The sound of a giggle from the other end of the line and then Joni hung up the receiver. Running upstairs to her bedroom she mentally went through the things she would need to take with her in her holdall – lip gloss, sun screen, sandals, costume. One by one they all got flung into the bag. Stopping for just a minute she decided to put the costume on under her clothes. It would cut down on the changing time at the beach – and she would be having a long cool dip in no time. Quickly she pulled it on, smoothed it down and taking one last look at her complexion in the mirror she flicked at her short blonde hair and smiled. Yes, she was right... Dick would love it. And if Jason was on the beach he might cast a couple of jealous looks her way. They had been an item once but had decided to split. In one way it had been for the best. Joni knew that. Somehow Jason and Joni hadn't brought out the best in each other. 'I don't know if he was that good an influence on me,' Joni mused as she pulled on her shorts and T-shirt once more. 'But Dick is lovely... and a good friend of Jason's. I think it's going to work out alright.'

But as Joni was just about to rush downstairs again her eye caught sight of the slightly worn Bible on her bedside table. She flicked a bit of dust off the cover. That didn't look good, she thought. How long was it since she had read it, really read it? Joni didn't care to count the days that had passed since she'd spent some time one on one with God in prayer and reading his word.

Only the other afternoon Joni had straddled the back of Tumbleweed her chestnut mare and looked across the wide panoramic view that surrounded the ranch. She had prayed then that God would turn her life around... the shallowness, the sin, the temptations. Joni had been fighting it all but losing spectacularly. The Bible lay there — a silent niggling reminder to the standards she couldn't keep and the life that she knew she was missing out on. There was something wrong. But right now there was a venue to prepare and a schedule to keep to — summer time fun. Perhaps a quick apologetic prayer would keep God happy and salve her conscience... but even in the middle of a good intention there was a loud knock on the kitchen door and a frantic call upstairs, 'Joni, are you ready yet? Butch is here already!'

Joni grabbed the beach bag — flicked at her hair one last time and ran out the door — the Bible would have to wait for another day and so would God.

***

Arriving at Chesapeake Bay it was still wonderfully warm. Butch parked the jeep close to the sands and with one arm full of provisions and the other round his new girlfriend Butch and Kathy headed off to set up the picnic site and then catch some sun. Kathy turned to Joni before heading off — 'We'll get the rest of the stuff later. If you want to go swimming I'll take your bag for you. We'll set up by those trees over there.'

Joni nodded, 'That's great. I said it would be mid to late afternoon before things really got started. Right now I'm going to cool off.' Joni stripped off her shorts and T-shirt and stuffed them inside the bag.

'Love the costume,' Kathy exclaimed. With a wink and a wave Joni handed Kathy her bag and shot off across the sand to a little outcrop of rocks by the edge of the water. 'These look just the right place for a dive,' Joni thought to herself.

A shiver went down Joni's spine as she anticipated the feeling of cool water skimming across her skin. A long cool soak was just what she needed. In the distance she could spot Butch spreading out a towel and Kathy sitting down beside him. Joni waved at the young lovers – Kathy waved back and then Joni edged out across the rocks to a large flat one – a perfect place to dive off. Kneeling down she splashed some surf across her body to cool herself before diving in. In the distance a couple of cars drew up and parked beside Butch's jeep. It was going to be a relaxing fun-packed afternoon at Chesapeake Bay. 'I'm going to enjoy this,' Joni thought... and then she dived.

***

The water was dark and murky, but Joni had dived there before many times and every time it had been the same. You sliced the water, sinking further, the flick of your toes against the surface told you that you were completely under – and then the weightless almost airborne feeling as you began an existence in this magical underwater world. But this other world was full of dangers if you didn't reach for the surface and force your head through to the oxygen and life above. Not that danger had entered Joni's thoughts for one moment... when you've done something a hundred times you don't stop to think on the one hundred and first. You only stop if something goes wrong.

And nothing appeared to be wrong as Joni's body began to slice the surface. In a split second the water's skin broke and she slipped beneath. Her arms outstretched, her legs taut, she waited to feel the sensation of her whole body skimming underneath the water – but something happened which changed everything.

The forward movement of Joni's body stopped and crumpled against something hard and unyielding. The sensation of the cool dark water disappeared in the darkness as other sensations took their place. Deep muffled sounds of something being dragged or perhaps rolling against the gravely sand. A loud electric buzzing went off in Joni's ear.

Joni heard these sounds, that felt like sensations yet, though she knew she had hit her head against something as she dived, she felt no pain.

Confused and disorientated Joni suddenly realised that her face was being rubbed against the crunching grinding sand at the bottom of the Bay.

'What's happening?' her thoughts screamed in the emptiness. 'I can't move. Am I caught in something?'

Floating amongst the debris of seaweed and sand small undercurrents lifted Joni slightly and dropped her further on, just a few steps, her body flopped then settled, flopped then settled drifting aimlessly across the bottom of Chesapeake Bay.

Light broke through the dark waters, picking out pieces of shell and coloured stones on the bottom of the Bay.

Joni's thoughts then suddenly cleared as the reality struck home of where she actually was.

'I need to get out. I need air. What's happened to me. Am I dead? No I can't be. I'm alive. I am alive. Oh God help!'

With that hurried frantic prayer pictures flooded Joni's head... her mother, her father, the people she loved – the things she had done, the things she hadn't done. Just then she heard a voice – muffled but puzzled sounding, breaking through the water, 'Joni? Joni?'

Two long tanned legs came towards her as the voice sounded out once again, but closer this time. 'Joni, what are you doing down there? Joni, are you looking for shells?'

It was Kathy! 'Kathy's here. She'll help. She'll know what to do.' Joni tried to struggle – but couldn't even do that. It was as if a weight on her body had trapped her, squashing her into the sand – tying her to the ebb and flow of the tide.

Joni's eyes rolled round in their sockets. She strained to look up and catch Kathy's eye, but not even her head could move where she wanted it to. All she could see was the dark shape of Kathy's shadow moving towards her across the shingle.

Soon the shadow was on top of her – but just then the darkness began to creep in. 'Oh please, God, don't let me die!' Joni's thoughts screamed.

Just then two strong arms reached down and grasped Joni on the shoulders. In the grappling, stumbling struggle Joni was lifted free of the water and... 'Oh, God, thank you, thank you!' She could breathe.

The anxious face of her sister looked down on Joni as she struggled to hold her above the water. 'Are you O.K.?' Kathy asked. The tone of her voice told Joni there was something wrong... very wrong... but Joni already knew that.

'Kathy,' Joni's voice cracked, 'I can't move. Why can't I move? My legs are stuck, my arms too. I can't move anything. Is there wire there or some net?'

But by this stage Kathy was taking charge, ordering curious onlookers to pull over their inflatable raft. 'Get that thing over here quick. You on shore call 911. We need the emergency services here... like now!'

Two young men swiftly paddled their raft over to where Kathy was struggling with Joni's weight in the water. Another was now running up the sands towards a phone kiosk by the road. Butch stood on the edge of the shore as Kathy and the two men gently laid Joni on the raft and pushed her across the water to the beach.

'Joni, what's wrong? Kathy was worried about you. You were under so long.' Butch leaned over the floating raft and looked at Joni with an anxious expression on his face. 'What were you doing out there? Fishing?' He laughed self-consciously but stopped as he saw Joni's pale face and the tears at the back of Kathy's eyes.

The raft scraped against the sand as it was pushed against the shore and it didn't take long before a crowd gathered. 'Get back everyone!' Kathy yelled. It seemed as if the beach party had started early and everyone was treating Joni as a sideshow. But Joni didn't recognise any of the faces and hated this feeling of being some sort of local curiosity. Anxious whispers and mutters sounded from the crowd. Joni tried to listen in but Kathy then started pushing people away. 'Move along with you and somebody call an ambulance!'

As the curious onlookers wandered away Butch kneeled down beside the inflatable raft and into Joni's line of vision. 'You O.K. kid?' he asked.

Joni couldn't nod, move her head or anything – all she could do was call out.

'Kathy. I can't move. I'm so scared. Kathy!'

Kathy was back at her side in an instant. 'It's all right, Joni, I'm here. It's going to be all right. You'll see.'

'Hold me please, Kathy. Hold me.'

'But I am, honey. I am.'

21

Just then the awful realisation hit Joni. 'I can't feel anything. Nothing at all.'

Kathy's face froze.

'Come on, Jon. Nothing? How about this?' She squeezed Joni's leg, hard.

'No, nothing,' Joni whispered.

'How about this then?' Kathy brushed her sister across the arm.

Panic rose in Joni. She whimpered, 'No. I tell you. I can't feel it. I can't feel anything.'

Kathy stopped, then reached her arm across Joni's chest to rest it on her sister's shoulder.

'How about that?'

Relief was written across Joni's face.

'Yes! Yes! I feel that!'

'Oh thank you Jesus. I'll be O.K.' Joni thought. 'I must have just hit my head in diving and the numbness will wear off in an hour or two hopefully.'

Wanting to reassure her sister Joni looked up at Kathy and smiled. 'It's going to be O.K. Don't worry. God won't let anything happen to me!'

But then the sirens sounded in the distance and grew louder as the ambulance pulled into the parking lot. Two paramedics appeared carrying a stretcher across the beach. Joni was lifted on top and carried across the sands. The plans and the dreams for a lovely summer's day evaporated. Just then Joni's statement became a question, 'God wouldn't let anything happen to me... would he?'

The doors closed, the siren sounded and the ambulance drove her away.

White Coats and Green Pastures

Kathy sat across from Joni's stretcher in the ambulance, giving worried but loving smiles, trying to calm Joni's anxious panic. But it kept rising despite all the assurances Joni gave herself that everything was going to be O.K.

'It'd be nice if these medic guys gave me a bit of reassurance,' Joni complained to herself. 'Not one of them has said anything to me since I've got in here.'

Joni strained her eyes round to see if she could catch a glimpse of what was going on outside in the normal world. The only part of the outside world she could see was what was immediately out the rear window. There was Butch carefully negotiating the late afternoon traffic in his silver coloured jeep. 'It was good of him to come with us. It'll mean that Kathy and I can get a lift home when this is all over,' thought Joni, relieved. 'At least that is one less thing to worry about… and Butch is bound to have phoned my parents. He might even drive them over and everything will be sorted out eventually.'

As the ambulance drove on through the streets, they passed houses, shopping malls, well-known street corners where Joni would usually hang out with her friends. Joni wondered if someone would think to tell Dick.

The hurried, anxious movements of the paramedics got in the way of Joni's limited view as they prepped the stretcher and patient for arrival.

'I wish one of them would stop just for a minute. Tell

me it's all going to be over soon. They're just going to check me over and then send me home right?'

Joni's train of thought was one way – all the time. 'This isn't serious – I'm going to be better soon – then we're going to go home.'

As the siren wail whined down to a silence the ambulance slowed down to a halt – a sign above the door said, 'Emergency Entrance. No Parking. Emergency Vehicles Only.'

Joni's stretcher was eased gently out of the ambulance doors and placed on top of a hospital trolley to be swiftly whisked into the emergency area. Kathy waved at Joni as she disappeared down the corridor. 'Mom and Dad will be here soon,' she called out and then she was gone.

The buzz of activity was frantic. Doctors and nurses moving everywhere. Half images flickered into Joni's gaze then out again as people moved at speed along disinfected corridors with smooth tiled floors. Joni's line of vision didn't see the whole picture as she stared permanently upwards.

Joni was then quickly wheeled into a hospital room. Bright white lights lit up everywhere in the room. The glare hurt her eyes but she couldn't move her face out of the way. It was then that she caught sight of shelves packed full of gauze, bandages and bottles. There were other shelves full of more sinister looking things such as scissors and scalpels, packets with long un-pronounceable names.

That morning Joni had been smelling the perfume of meadow-sweet on the air as she had taken Tumbleweed for a morning trot round the paddock. Now all she could smell was disinfectant, the smell of stringent hygiene and medical cleanliness.

That morning she'd been mucking out the stables

listening to the sound of her chestnut mare kicking up her hooves and whinnying with delight at a new morning. Joni was now listening to urgent voices, distant sirens and the continual swish and swing of hospital doors.

That morning Joni had stood in front of the mirror smiling at her own reflection, day dreaming about her perfect day at the beach... a new day, a new boyfriend, a new costume. Now she was living in the middle of a nightmare and she just wanted this day to end... no... she wished it had never begun.

Just as Joni was trying once again to get some movement out of her body two nurses entered the room, one held a clipboard, the other pulled the privacy curtains around Joni.

'Can you tell me what's wrong?' Joni asked. Voicing her anxieties seemed to unlock something she had been keeping clamped shut since Chesapeake Bay. Tears began to prick the backs of her eyes. The nurse just shrugged her shoulders and went about her business, removing Joni's rings and other jewellery. Joni felt the moist tears trickle down her face into her ears. It didn't matter what question Joni asked, neither nurse seemed eager to answer. 'Perhaps they just don't know,' Joni thought. But at the back of her mind was the concern, 'Maybe they just don't want to tell me yet.'

'What are you doing with my jewellery?' Joni then asked.

Showing her a small, labelled envelope with Joni's name on it the nurse sighed, 'I'm putting it in this envelope see? It's *regulations*.' This word would become very familiar to Joni before the evening was through.

'How long do I have to stay here?'

'Ask the doctor. It's regulations.'

'Will I be able to go home tonight?'

'The doctor will be here soon. Ask him. It's regulations.'

'What are you doing with these scissors?'

'I'm cutting off your swimsuit. It's regulations.'

'What! You're what! It's brand new! I just got it last week. Please…'

'Sorry – it's regulations.'

And with that the large scissors began to chop roughly through the shimmering electric blue swimming costume.

That morning Joni had been admiring it as she took it out from the drawer thinking about how much Dick would like it. Now the evening was drawing to a close and the costume lay in strips and scraps over the floor of the disinfected treatment room.

Joni's tears came quick and fast. She was lying naked on a hospital trolley. There were no friends or family with her. 'Do my parents even know I am here?' Joni couldn't even move an arm to try and cover herself. None of the nurses had even noticed that the sheet had slipped off her chest – exposing Joni's nakedness for all to see.

As she lay there answering questions, undergoing examinations, letting surgeons and doctors prod her and stick her with pins, Joni remembered some words from her childhood, words that her father had taught her.

> *"The Lord is my shepherd I shall not want.*
> *He maketh me to lie down in green pastures.*
> *He restores my soul.*
> *Yea though I walk through the valley of the shadow of death*
> *I will fear no evil for thou art with me."*

'I want you God. I really do. I want you to stop this. I'm lying down here – but I want to walk away. Why can't I move? Please God, do something. Please God, make it be all right. Restore me. Make me better. Just make it stop. Please. You say that you're with me but how can I tell that? Are you really with me? Are you really there at all? Or are you just something my parents have told me about? I need to know if you are real or if I'm just talking to a hospital ceiling.'

And as the hospital staff talked over her, mumbling words such as 'fracture dislocation' and 'fourth and fifth cervical level', Joni continued to stare at the ceiling.

***

Later that evening Joni heard someone bark an order. 'Get her O-R prepped then and someone try and reach her parents.'

'O-R prepped? What's that?' Joni wondered, 'And I was sure they'd have reached Mom and Dad by now? But... hey... what's she doing? That nurse has just stuck a needle in my vein. What's happening? Oh dear that noise... what's going on?'

A loud whining noise was sounding out from somewhere to Joni's left. Joni strained her eyes and in the corner of her vision she saw one of the doctors holding in his hands a pair of clippers.

'Clippers?' Joni thought she was mistaken at first. 'What does he think he's going to do with those?'

Briskly he moved towards her. 'Yes,' Joni thought. 'These are definitely clippers... hair clippers.' Then she realised what they were going to do.

'Oh no! Please no! Not my hair.' But as the locks of sunkissed blonde hair fell in clumps to the floor another more terrifying sound split the air. 'Is that a drill?'

Joni, doped and befuddled by the drugs that the nurse had just injected into her arm, began to slip into unconsciousness... but the terror still lingered.

'I'm falling asleep. What if I never wake up? I might not see Dick again? Kathy? Mom? Dad?... Oh God, help me. I'm afraid.'

Then nothing. Joni was unconscious and the operation began.

Afterwards the days and nights merged into one long drug induced haze. Occasionally Joni would fight her way through the fog of drugs and confusion to try and stay awake to be in the real world... but it would be a momentary struggle before her mind succumbed to the drugs once again. But then sometimes she would come to instantly, in a terrifying moment she would be awake in the middle of the confusing noises and chaos of a busy hospital ward. In blind terror she would start screaming, 'Stop drilling, stop drilling – please just stop, stop...' – a quiet comforting voice would soon soothe her fears and then she would realise that the drilling was only the whining, and clattering of the air conditioning unit.

Sharp pains pierced through Joni's skull. Where before she had been able to move her face slightly now she was stuck fast. Large metal tongs attached to a spring cable device seemed to be trying to pull her head away from the rest of her body. It was too much to take in, particularly as her mind was in a constant swing between the terrifying reality of hospital and the confusing world of hallucination and surreal dreams. Joni's eyes would close as more drugs pumped through her body. As she drifted off friends and family would drift into her visions and nightmares. When she'd wake up she would sometimes find herself upside down with her head facing the floor, other times facing the ceiling. These confusing, disorientating positions were terrifying at first. But she soon realised that she was actually attached to the bed by a canvas frame and in this way was suspended above the ground, the tongs still drilled into her head. It was a strange position and Joni wasn't entirely sure why she had to lie like this but while Joni remained awake she soon got used to seeing people's feet and legs rather than their faces.

Some went quietly about their business, others took the time to answer Joni's questions as gradually she became more aware of her surroundings.

Nurses and doctors moved around the ward discussing, quietly, various medical problems and situations. Joni soon learned that she wasn't in a bed... but something called a Stryker frame. Nurses explained the procedure to her and at best Joni thought it sounded as though she was strapped into a canvas sandwich. Every two hours Joni would have to be flipped from the face up position to the face down. Placing a canvas frame on top of her one nurse would hold the weights that were attached to the tongs on Joni's head and flip her 180 degrees so that she would now be facing the opposite way.

It was either floor or ceiling. Not exactly a room with a view — just two distinctly boring ones. But initially Joni wasn't concerned about boredom or lack of variety, not when she was fighting for her very life.

It wasn't that long before Joni learned that she was actually in ICU with other patients — an intensive care unit for the seriously ill or injured. Though she couldn't see the other patients she was aware of their presence as she heard their groans and the beeping of their machines. Soon she was picking out the sounds of individual patients and hospital staff. One particular morning Joni was flipped in the face down position and asked a pair of nylon stockings passing by what the noise was in the corner of the room.

'Oh that?' the nurse replied. 'That's Tom's resuscitation equipment. He was in a diving accident like you and broke his neck. But he can't breathe on his own without help. That's what you're hearing … his breathing apparatus.'

Joni felt a tug on her heart. Here was a young man who had experienced the same thing she had. 'He knows what I've been through and I certainly know what he's been through.' An idea sprung into Joni's mind. 'Nurse?'

'Yes.'

'Could you write him a note from me, just to say hi?'

'Sure. What a good idea. He'll love it. I'll say it's from the pretty young blonde in Stryker frame Two. That will really perk him up!'

Joni giggled, 'Just say it's from Joni… but on second thoughts… you should tell him I'm a girl. Most people get my name confused and think I'm a guy. I'm kind of named after my Dad you see.'

'Yeah, well I'll say its from Joni – the pretty young blonde female in Stryker frame Two. What should I write?'

'Oh, how about. Hi, hang on in there. Joni.'

And that was the beginning of several notes that made their way back and fore across the ICU floor over the next few days.

Joni would wake up during the night to hear Tom's resuscitation equipment breathing for him and would wonder what he looked like and if he was finding it difficult to sleep too. One night she decided she would ask him for a photograph the next day… but she never did.

Later on as Joni tried to get back to sleep a sudden silence broke into the ward. The resuscitator had stopped. Nurses rushed to Tom's bedside and orders were shouted for a new resuscitator 'Immediately.'

Footsteps ran down the tiled hallway and a voice requested urgent emergency help on the telephone. Joni had never felt so helpless. It was a crisis. If nothing happened soon they would lose him.

'Tom! Tom! Can you hear me?' a doctor called.

With the other respirator on another floor the staff had to keep up mouth-to-mouth resuscitation. Some moments later the equipment arrived but then it was too late. 'We've lost him. He's dead.'

Joni sobbed. 'Tom's dead.' The horror struck home. A friend she had never seen or spoken to had died. Then the sudden realisation hit her, 'If it happened to Tom why not me?'

Later the next day a nurse tried to calm Joni's fears.

'You're not on a respirator, Joni, remember?'

'Yeah I know but I'm dependant on other things – my IV (intravenous solutions) they like feed me don't they? And the catheter well that drains my body of wastes and poisons?'

'Correct. Full marks, Joni Eareckson on IVs and catheters. But what are you getting at?'

'Well what if one of those fail? I'd be in just as much trouble.'

'Look, Joni,' the nurse said consolingly. 'We're going to take good care of you!'

But as others in the ward died, some with injuries just like Joni's, she couldn't help but wonder if the medical staff were just hiding things from her.

'Perhaps they know I'm going to die but they're just afraid to tell me.'

Joni closed her eyes tight. 'I'd rather know. If they're hiding things from me – I wish they wouldn't. Nobody's ever hidden things from me before. Even as a kid I was just like the other girls – a four year old on the back of a horse. Some people would say it was mad... but that was the Eareckson girls for you ... horse mad and ready for anything. They never sheltered me in that way... they just helped me tackle anything!'

Joni let her mind drift back to days when all she'd had to worry about was a stubborn pony and keeping up with her big sisters.

Before it all Began

'Joni, come on. Don't look down. Show him who's boss. Don't let a horse feel your fear. Focus on me. That's right. Focus – now push him. Yes. Go on, girl. Yes, well done!'

Ten year old Joni, with gritted teeth and an anxious grip of the reins and saddle had just defeated a battle with her nerves and her stubborn little piebald mare... and then there was the river in full flow, with the occasional rock and floating debris thrown in – just a typical pony trek for the Eareckson girls.

Joni had been determined to go on this trek with her older sisters, and they hadn't disagreed. If Joni was up for it she could come with them. She'd have to take her own gear, and pull her own weight and at all times she must keep up with them. 'If you slow us down we just won't take you the next time.'

But Joni was determined to keep up. Nothing was going to stop her. Even though the pace of the trek was faster than she'd originally thought and her horse was finding it difficult to keep up with the taller and stronger mounts of her sisters, Joni soldiered on. Giving up was just not her style. Struggling on, Joni didn't complain as there was no way she was going to get her sisters to turn back for anything. But the river had caused a problem – a big one – and as Joni found herself and her mount in the middle of it she realised that perhaps she had bitten off more than she could chew.

'Move along there – get – go on,' she urged as the horse

floundered in the strong current. 'Come on you silly thing – get a grip. It's not that hard. We've crossed rivers like this before. Move along!' But quietly in the back of Joni's mind was the nagging thought, 'Perhaps now is the time to shout for help. Jay and the others are still close enough to hear me. They can't have gone that far.'

However, Joni had too much pride to cry for help. But thankfully Jay had turned her mount round to tell Joni to get a shift on when she realised that her little sister wasn't there. Cantering back to the river she came across Joni in the middle of the foaming waters – in more than a spot of difficulty.

Jay could easily have got in there and pulled Joni's mount out – taking control of the horse and her sister. But a little bit of patience and wisdom made her realise that this was something Joni could and would manage herself. She just needed a bit of encouragement and advice. If there had ever been a family born in the saddle it had been the Earecksons – and Joni was an Eareckson through and through.

With the right words and the right encouragement Joni soon had her horse up the bank and onto solid ground. A smile spread from ear to ear. She had done it. She was on the trek again.

Linda, Jay, Kathy and Joni, the four daughters of John and Margaret Eareckson were accomplished horse women almost as soon as they could ride a bike, if not before. And that morning Jay looked proud as her little sister sat well in the saddle and seemed quite relaxed now despite her ordeal. 'Yes girl,' she smiled at Joni. 'Us Earecksons sure know how to ride. Gee up then. Let's catch up with the others at the crossing.'

And with that the two sisters built their speed up into a canter and went on their way.

Sitting that night at the camp fire Joni let her eyes gently close as the other Eareckson girls chatted away about boys and proms and summer beach barbeques. It had been a wonderful day and was just another one to add to the increasing number of Eareckson expeditions that her family had chalked up over the years.

'I suppose I've been in the saddle for as long as I've been able to walk,' Joni muttered to herself. 'Dad loves to tell me how he put me in the saddle at two years old. And then when I was only four the family trekked over a hundred miles from Laramie to Cheyenne. I was the youngest ever to ride the Cheyenne trail.'

Opening up her eyes again Joni gazed at the countless number of stars above her. 'There have been so many star-filled nights and mountain trecks for us. As far back as I can remember we've had camp fires and trail rides, family times – times like this.' Joni smiled as she looked at her older sisters who were now busy talking about the good points and bad points of several eligible young men that they knew.

'Huh,' Joni whispered quietly to the snuffling horses preparing to go to sleep. 'I don't care what those girls think, there's none of those guys who can hold a candle to our dad.' And with that Joni snuggled down under her blanket, shut her eyes for good this time and dreamed of home – a little stone built house that had been started and finished by her father with salvaged sail ship beams and discarded stone masonry. It was the perfect home for a growing family as John Eareckson was the perfect man to build it. Practical, good with his hands and a real honest-to-goodness hard worker.

***

The Eareckson family ranch had been a pure labour of love. It was the proof in stones and mortar that John Eareckson loved the young woman who had agreed to become his bride and who would bring up his family... and he loved her with all his heart. When the world seemed to be falling about their ears – crashing stockmarkets, a national financial crisis – John was still determined that his family would have a place to call home – a place of their own.

'Those days were hard days,' he'd remind his family when they asked him yet again to tell the story of how he and Mom had met.

'It was the depression. Money and work were scarce, and when your Mom had the good sense to fall for me,' at that point he'd wink and smile, 'well I just had to show her how much I loved her. She'd agreed to marry me so I agreed to build us a love nest!' At that point if Joni's mom was in the room she would blush and smile and laugh a little. Joni and the other girls would giggle – but the love nest had been built and that had been the beginning of the Eareckson family.

It had been such a lot of hard work. Boulders shifted by hand, foundations dug, beams raised, roofs slated. Everything was done by John Eareckson himself. His family meant that much to him, even before they were born. His girls... and the 'little un', Joni, who was called after him were all precious in his sight.

Even though it did cause her a lot of hassle at school Joni didn't wish for any other name. She went through life spelling it and explaining that it wasn't a boy's name. 'Do I look like a boy to you?'

But despite the life time of name spelling Joni was proud

to be called after the man in her life. But it wasn't long before Dad's place as the main man in her life wasn't as exclusive as it had once been. High school beckoned and with that came athletics, lacrosse and boyfriends.

***

'Come on, Mom, you just gotta let me go.'

Joni wheedled away at her mother who stood at the kitchen sink looking slightly puzzled.

'Well, Joni Eareckson, it's hard to keep up with you these days. Weren't you going to try out for the Lacrosse team next weekend?'

'No, Mom! That's not till the weekend after… and I'm a cert for the team anyway. We know that.'

Mrs Eareckson smiled at the confidence of her now teenage daughter. Joni had grown up so quickly over the last few years. It hardly seemed any time since she'd been the little ten year old playing 'catch up' to all her big sisters… now she was a hop, skip and a jump away from being a woman. Joni's complete love of life and her energy was infectious and as Joni's mother thought about the proposed weekend she agreed that a weekend away with some young Christians would be good for Joni.

'Well, I'm not so sure about the fact that you just "gotta go"… but seeing as it's with Christians and good things are said of this Young Life group … well if your father agrees…'

Joni squealed in excitement and before her mother had finished the sentence Joni was jumping around the kitchen in delight. 'Oh I can't wait. It's going to be great. Everyone's going to be there!'

'Everyone? Did you hear that Mom?' Jay smiled. 'How

do you suppose they're going to be able to fit them all into that campsite? Last time I looked there were hundreds of kids at Woodlawn High.'

'Hmm,' Joni's mum smiled, 'I think you know what Joni means, dear.'

'Yeah I do. In Joni speak "everyone" means "all the cool kids".'

Joni smiled at their little joke and then just hugged herself with glee. Mrs Eareckson laughed, 'I just wish all the cool kids had been Christians when I went to school.' But as she turned round to smile again at her youngest daughter she was nowhere to be seen. Joni couldn't hold out any longer and had run out to the yard to speak to her father. She knew he would let her go. The Young Life weekend was going to be the event of the year – miss it and you missed out – big time! The news around the student campus was that it was going to be fantastic.

Later that night, snuggled up in her little room, the covers tucked under her chin, Joni could feel the excitement welling up inside her.

'Dad was pleased I wanted to go. I knew that though,' Joni remembered his broad smile and the twinkle in his eye when she'd told him.

'Course you can go, hon,' he'd laughed. 'But boy that takes me back. It doesn't seem like yesterday when I was taking youngsters like you on camping trips. I used to take your mother out on dates and the whole youth group would tag along too. But don't you go getting any ideas,' he said in a mock warning. 'There's plenty of time for boyfriends yet – you're still young.'

Joni had rolled her eyes to the barn ceiling … boyfriends, as if. But as Joni dreamed and planned about the weekend .

38

to come she did wonder about which of the boys would be there. Quickly she tried to work out what the boy/girl ratio would be but felt a bit sheepish when she remembered that it was a Christian weekend she was going to – so she picked up her Bible instead. 'You're not going there to flirt,' she admonished herself, 'but it might be fun,' she giggled.

However, as Joni packed her rucksack the following weekend she had no way of knowing that this weekend would be the beginning of something big. When the campfires and songs were just memories there would be one incident that would always be more than a memory – it would be a beginning.

Arriving at the large campsite the girls were shown their dorms and the boys were taken to one of the other dorms. A quick look told you who was here and who wasn't.

'Jason's here,' a girl whispered in Joni's ear.

'Yes, I see that.'

'Well I've heard him say that he thinks you're cute.'

'So what. Every girl in this campsite is cute… and we don't want to start something this weekend and regret it later. It's a Christian weekend we're on… so…'

'We're here to do more than read our Bibles and pray Joni Eareckson… at least I am.' And the pretty little brunette tossed her hair and looked across the yard. 'Oh, there's Dwight. See you later Joni.' And she was gone.

Joni sighed, 'Perhaps I'm being silly. You've gotta have fun on these things. After all that's why I've been pestering Mom to let me go. The Young Life events are fantastic. Everyone says that you really enjoy yourself. So lighten up Joni and don't take things too seriously,' she said to herself.

But that evening Joni met someone for the first time – who changed everything. There were plenty of guys around for sure – good looking ones too – and Jason did keep smiling at her. But when Joni settled down to listen to her first seminar at Natural Bridge, Virginia, everyone took second place to the one she met during the talk.

That night Carl Nelson held the group spell bound in silence. They listened – really listened to his talk on the Ten Commandments.

'Think about God's glory and righteousness guys. That's the standard – the perfect standard and that is expressed through the Ten Commandments. It's impossible to reach heaven by trying to stick to a list of moral do's and don'ts. There's just no way any one of us can live up to those commandments that God has laid down.'

Joni sat almost frozen to the spot. As the meeting broke up she shook herself and decided that she needed some fresh air. The heat in the room was stifling but something else was bothering her.

'I'm a sinner,' she thought as she wandered out into the darkness, the sound of cheerful chatter fading away in the building behind her. Walking further on she was surprised that she had never really understood the astonishing fact before. 'I suppose I've never really thought that much about God's perfection, until tonight that is. I just don't stand up to the comparison. He's like perfect and I'm – well I'm a sinner.'

There it was again, the startling, unavoidable fact. 'A lost sinner at that,' Joni muttered.

It wasn't as though she'd lived long enough to chalk up decades of misdeeds, thoughtless words and lustful thoughts – just one sin was enough to banish her from God's presence, from heaven. Joni remembered Carl's words.

'It's impossible to reach heaven by trying to stick to a list of moral do's and don'ts.'

Joni took that statement and mulled over it a bit in her head. The obvious conclusion was soon arrived at,

'I can't save myself. So who...?'

It was in the very act of asking that small question that Joni came to the biggest answer of her life.

'That's why Jesus came!' she gasped. 'Jesus is God in the flesh. He came to fulfil the law – to keep all the do's and don'ts that I just can't! He lived the perfect life and when he died he was paying the penalty and taking the punishment that should have been mine! Oh! I understand now!'

With that Joni bowed her head beneath the myriad of stars and prayed. 'Oh, Lord Jesus, thank you.' Then, leaning back against the bark of an old sycamore tree, Joni looked up again. 'I see my sin now, God, and I see your mercy. Thank you for sending your son to die for me. Please take charge of my life – I don't want to disappoint you anymore.'

That night in the dorm Joni was excitedly gossiping to girl friends about how she'd met ... not the new boyfriend as she had once dreamed about ... but Jesus.

'It's just amazing. How did I not understand it before?' Joni shrugged her shoulders as her friends looked on. 'I mean, that Jesus died for me, personally. Me! Joni Eareckson.'

The young brunette with her hair tied back in pigtails burrowed deeper into her sleeping bag.

'Well, we all know that Joni. And you've been to Sunday school along with the rest of us. We've all heard what you're saying and it's not like news or anything!'

Joni wrinkled her forehead slightly and nodded. 'I can see what you're getting at but I've known the information since kindergarten and it's only right now that I really understand what it all means. It is as if there's two kinds of knowing – one is a knowing inside your head and the other is a knowing inside your heart.'

'Hmm, I suppose that kind of makes sense. But what I don't get is what all this abundant life stuff is that they keep going on about and how God is going to give it to us! Is he really? And what exactly will it be?'

Joni smiled from ear to ear. 'I'm not too sure about that either but the way I feel right now I can't wait – God's sure got good things in store for me. I can just feel it.'

And as Joni got ready, a few days later, to head off to the farm for the rest of her summer vacation, she wondered if Jason Leverton might feature in God's fun plans for her future. As she turned to give him a last smile and a wave her heart skipped a beat.

'See you, Joni,' he hollered. With one bronzed muscular arm he ran his hand through his thick mop of sandy coloured hair.

'Yeah, see you,' Joni cried back out the window of the bus. 'Does he really mean it?' she wondered. She hoped so.

The little brunette smiled at her as the bus drove off, 'So you find God and a boyfriend at Young Life camp. I told you it would be a good weekend,' and she laughed.

Joni smiled, she didn't know about the boyfriend. But she did know about God… and she knew who she was taking home… and who really mattered at the end of it all. 'Thank you, Jesus,' she whispered as the bus turned round the corner and headed off back to Maryland.

When Life is Like a Punchbag

She needn't have worried. Jason didn't just see Joni he started dating her. It was a summer full of socials, treks, picnics and a wedding or two for good measure. And then when the summer was over it was back to High school and senior year for Joni. But it wasn't all books and tests this year... Joni smiled to herself... at least she could be sure of a date to the prom. That was one less thing to worry about.

Mucking out the stables early one morning Jay came over to stand beside her sister, with a quizzical look on her face. 'You really like this guy don't you?'

'Does it show?' Joni laughed.

'I'll say,' Jay replied. 'You're walking around shovelling horse manure with a smile as big as a slice of watermelon on your face.' Jay shovelled another forkful of manure out into the yard.

Joni took a breather and leaned against the old, stone wall. 'Things sure seem to be going well between Jason and you then,' Jay looked Joni in the eye – a twinkle lurked there. Jay was going to get some gossip out of her little sister eventually.

Joni just stood there and smiled some more. Jay took a deep breath and went on, 'Saw you headed up to the park the other afternoon. It's nice and quiet up there isn't it?'

Joni nodded and reached out for one of the hard bristled brooms to sweep up the remaining pieces of straw. 'Hmm, nice and quiet. That's right.'

Jay put down the fork against the stable door and hands on hips exclaimed, 'Come on Jon – sisters are supposed to share everything don't you know and that includes secrets… I see I'm just going to have to… tickle it out of you!'

And with that the two girls ran squealing away from the stables towards the kitchen door.

A couple of older and wiser eyes looked on from behind the farm window. Joni's mother sighed. It wasn't that big a problem in one way – but something was niggling her. She would have to have that conversation with Joni. She couldn't put it off any longer. In one way it might be easier just to leave everything as it was. Joni's temperament lately had been a bit erratic. She was growing up and discovering feelings and emotions that were new and bewildering. Joni's snappish come backs were getting more and more frequent when her parents tried to take her from the wrong path on to the right one. It was hard to give advice when it wasn't really wanted but Mrs Eareckson knew that if they didn't talk about Jason then something might happen that could lead to a whole lot of trouble later on.

As the laughing, gasping girls opened the door and left their riding boots in the yard, Mrs Eareckson called out that they were to get themselves cleaned up and ready for breakfast. On second thoughts Joni's talk would be better if left until tonight, but no later.

That evening, after chores were done, Joni was brushing her teeth before heading to bed. A gentle knock was heard on the bathroom door. 'Joni love, can I have a word?'

'Sure Mom, I'm just brushin' my teeth. I'll be down in a second.'

'O.K. sweetheart. Come to my room when you're done.'

Soon both mother and daughter were sat on the edge of Mr and Mrs Eareckson's large wooden bed. The patchwork quilt neatly folded, hung over the bed posts. A bouquet of dried roses were placed on a window seat, wafting the subtle smell of petals around the room. A couple of basic beauty items lay on the dresser – but nothing more. Joni flopped herself on top of the mattress and looked up into her mother's pale blue eyes.

'What's up, Mom?' Joni asked a bit suspiciously.

'I'm not going to keep you long, honey, as I know you'll understand why I'm asking you to do this. You may not agree, but as your mother, I only want what is best for you, hon.'

Joni let a sigh escape from her throat slowly, 'Right then, what have I done now?' she said.

'Well dear there's a young man standing outside your window. He's been there for the last three nights in a row and I know you've been breaking our curfew to shimmy down the drain pipe to meet him.'

Joni's face went a little pale. She'd been discovered! Now she was for it.

Mrs Eareckson continued, 'You know that this is against Eareckson family rules, rules that have been set up by your father and me for your own safety. Your father is at this very moment sending him on his way. Now, Joni, don't sulk,' Mrs Eareckson admonished. Joni's face had a rather petulant scowl on it and her body language showed that she wasn't best pleased with this turn of events. But Mrs Eareckson continued, 'You know how much your Dad likes Jason – they like nothing better than a good wrestling match and talking about sport – and we're more than happy to have him round to the farm and to see you going out together.

He's a good Christian boy and I know we can trust you. But don't try and see how far you can go. Rules are rules. From tonight there will be no more meetings past curfew. Do you understand?'

Joni nodded, the slightly sullen look on her face beginning to fade. 'Is that all?' she asked her mother quietly. Mrs Eareckson nodded her head and Joni slunk off to bed. Her mother only stayed a moment before going over to check if she was O.K. A little tear had trickled down Joni's face, but it was soon kissed away. 'Sweet heart. I'm not punishing you. I'm protecting you. I know what it's like to be a teenage girl and I know that there are more temptations for you than there ever was for me. I'm concerned that if we don't watch you and help you to fight these temptations yourself... well in the heat of the moment you and Jason could find yourselves letting your emotions get the better of you. You know what I'm trying to say, Joni.'

Joni sighed, 'Yes Mom, I know. I should be keeping myself pure for marriage.'

'You both should, Jason too. And night time meetings behind your parents' backs... that could lead from one thing to another and you could end up in a physical relationship that is against God's word.'

As Joni's mom tucked her in, Joni closed her eyes and pretended to fall into a deep sleep. 'What Mom said is true. I realise that. But Mom doesn't know how well I understand it.' Lately Joni and Jason's quiet park dates had turned into long hikes through the woods and meadows and intimate meetings in quiet secluded spots. Joni knew that Jason and she were not following God's law because every time they met ... it was just getting too close. Joni knew that something had to be done. But not yet... not just yet. It was just so hard living life like a punch bag with your body saying one thing and your conscience the other.

But some time later a quiet date led again to the two young people trying to cope with a passion that they could hardly control.

'This isn't right, Jason,' Joni gasped pulling away from him. 'We don't want to disobey God but we are and when we do we both feel so guilty. We say we believe in God but we're not doing what he says. What does that make us?'

'Yeah I know, Joni, I know. I keep asking the question, "How do I keep my ways pure, God?" There is only one answer – by obeying his word. We've been disobeying it.'

Joni sighed, 'We've got to stop seeing each other, Jason. It's the only way.'

'Yeah, and then some other guy is going to be dating you and… well I'll get jealous and who knows what he is going to be like. If you're going to date anyone else, Joni make sure he's a better Christian than me.'

Joni reached out a comforting hand… but then thought better of it. Jason kicked some dirt with the toe of his boot and then cleared his throat, 'My mate Dick would be a good guy for you to hang out with.'

At first Joni thought it a little strange to be breaking up with one boy and then going out with his best mate… but Jason thought it was a good idea … and Dick well, he was every bit as good looking as Jason. But Joni thought sternly to herself as she waved goodbye to Jason at the edge of the meadow, 'If anything happens with this new guy I'm going to make sure this whole romance thing doesn't get out of control.'

Senior year went on, Dick proved a good boy to have around and Joni knew in one way he was a better influence on her that Jason had been. Dick, in one way, was a strong rock that she could cling to and his influence seemed to be bringing out some better emotions. Her Bible study and prayer times became more serious and from one angle Joni could almost say that perhaps her life was falling into shape. But Dick's deep blue eyes and his gorgeous smile could still send her legs to jelly... and she knew she wasn't the only one who felt that way. That was another emotion Joni was fighting against – Jealousy. Joni could one moment be emotionally stable and then the next be in the middle of an emotional storm.

One morning, graduation over and the summer holidays just begun, some post arrived for Joni Eareckson. Joni had just spent an energetic morning in the paddock with Tumbleweed, doing some jumps and practice for the summer riding events that were coming up. She'd trekked a few miles over the surrounding hills and had let her mind dwell on some of the deeper things of life. As she anticipated what her life would bring she kept wondering about why she still didn't feel satisfied. Something was wrong... and she prayed to God about it. 'If you don't turn things around, God, I don't know what is going to happen. You have to do something.'

And then when she frantically opened the brown manila envelope that her mother handed to her at the kitchen table her heart was in her throat – had she managed to get in? Had her grades been good enough despite the slacking? 'Yes!' Joni yelled. 'I've been accepted for Maryland! My grades were good enough thankfully.' But Joni knew that they could have been better, a lot better.

'Well done, sweet heart.' Both her parents came over to give their little girl a hug.

Her sisters came over to give their congratulations and friends phoned to compare results and squeal about how thrilling it would be to go to college together. That night, around a celebratory meal, Joni looked at her friends and family laughing and joking together.

'This is it,' Joni thought to herself. 'I've got the friends, the boyfriend and the college place. It's great. Life's great... but why, God do I feel as though something is seriously wrong? If you don't turn things around, God, I don't know where I'll be headed. You've got to really work in my life. You have to do something.'

Just then a bunch of young school friends came over to chat with Joni. 'They say a heat wave's coming. Chesapeake Bay is going to be the place to hang out this summer.' Joni nodded in agreement. 'Yeah. I love the summer picnics we have there. Diving off the dinghies. Swimming in the surf.'

'Tell you what,' someone interrupted. ''How about a celebratory beach party. All the guys who are heading off to college this fall – we'll all get together – get a picnic organised, a barbeque.'

Joni smiled, a party sounded great. It might shift this funny feeling that had been hounding her all week. 'That's cool. Tell you what – if we all bring something, I'll phone round some of the others. We'll do it next week – Kathy's desperate to introduce you all to her new boyfriend – his name's Butch and he's got a jeep.'

'Cool, get him to take some drinks and we've got this party sorted.'

And as the old school friends parted with waves and calls of, 'See you next week!' Joni looked forward to a good summer.

***

'But it only took a moment and everything changed,' Joni screwed up her eyes as two nurses spun her Stryker frame round to face the floor once again. 'I said that God wouldn't let anything happen to me... but he has... and I just don't understand why!'

I'm Walking out of Here!

It seemed as though every day had some new piece of advice or information to be absorbed and taken in. Some of it was medical involving words such as 'total quadriplegia' and 'diagonal fractures'. Occasionally words would crop up time and time again such as 'fourth and fifth cervical levels.' These conversations however meant very little to Joni – as all she wanted to know was if she had a broken neck and if she was going to die like the guy she had read about in 'Black Beauty'.

'He fell from his horse and broke his neck,' Joni remembered, and a panic began to rise in her throat until she flung the thought away and concentrated on what she was going to do when she got out of here.

The thought of death was one that was almost too difficult to deal with – eventually Joni decided it was better not to listen to the white coats and she simply began to switch off whenever their conversations became too frightening.

But not all of the medical staff talked science – others seemed to assume that as a patient she should only be told on a need to know basis – and as far as they were concerned she didn't really need to know very much. 'You'll be fine. You're doing great.' Comments like this were almost as bad as the terrifying words she didn't understand.

The few things that kept Joni going were the visits from her family and friends... but even those treasured visits seemed to result in conflicting and opposite emotions. It was wonderful to have Mom and Dad coming in – their presence was often calming and a great source of comfort – but it hurt Joni to see their anxious faces and to see them scrabbling around on the floor to speak to her when her frame was flipped down.

Dick too was more than a good friend. The two teenagers were still very much in love. The accident hadn't changed Dick's feelings. It certainly hadn't changed Joni's. She would cling to every anticipated visit, every kiss, every longing look that they would share when he came to visit. Dick was strong for both of them, though Joni could see how much he was hurting too. Tears would well up in his eyes as he suffered with Joni through her heartache, pain and bewilderment. But there were moments of fun and laughter too… Dick made sure that there were.

One evening Joni gasped as Dick rushed in the ward door and scrabbled onto the floor flushed and just a bit guilty looking. Joni noticed that he was wearing a jacket. 'Dick – isn't it a bit hot to be wearing that?'

Dick laughed and his chest wriggled. 'Yes. That jacket definitely wriggled,' Joni thought as she looked again, staring at the thick baseball jacket. Was that something forcing its way out through the zipper? 'Dick, what have you done?' Joni gasped as a little brown and white puppy leaped out of his jacket and frantically began licking at Joni's face. 'Oh he's so cute. How on earth did you get him past the gestapo at the hospital entrance?'

'Well,' Dick winked slyly, 'It helps if you know where there's a back stairway and a handy exit. But nine floors – with this little pooch – I'm telling you. It wasn't easy.'

Anita, one of Joni's favourite nurses, pushed open the

swing door into Joni's room. She looked across at the pair of teenagers and took everything in and laughed. 'I haven't seen a thing.' The puppy yelped. 'There aren't any puppies here! I must be imagining things!' and with a wink and a wave Anita moved on to the next ward. Her relaxed attitude meant that friends were treated like family, and family visits stretched well beyond the hospital limits. She even spent time reading Joni some of her favourite poetry. All these little things went some way to making Joni's stay in hospital better or at least more bearable. But Joni's questions and spiritual battle were a long, long, way from any conclusion.

'There just didn't seem to be any answers,' Joni struggled with her doubts. 'Why has this accident happened to me? But I don't care what anyone says I am going to walk out of here. I am!' Throughout it all Joni doggedly grasped the ultimate hope that she was going to walk out, on her own two legs... that sooner, rather than later, everything would be back to normal. 'I'm going to get my legs back, my arms are going to work again, I'm going to go to college with Dick and one day we'll get married. I know we will. God's going to heal me. I'm going to get out of this. I'm walking out of here!'

And it seemed one morning, to Joni at least, that this was going to happen. The news from the doctor seemed good, and her parents also seemed encouraged. Joni could tell by their faces. 'It's great news isn't it, Mom,' Joni gushed. 'Fusion surgery – they're going to put my bones back together. Then I'll be able to walk.' And then when the surgery was over and Joni was wheeled into a new ward she read this as another sign that things were changing for the better. After all if she was no longer in the ICU ward then the surgery must have been a success. Joni's heart thrilled when the surgeon came in to visit with her parents and her the following day, 'The surgery was a success — everything went fine,' was his diagnosis.

A silent exultant prayer jumped from Joni's heart, 'I knew it would. I knew God wouldn't let anything happen to me. I wonder when I'll be able to walk?'

'But what I'm most concerned about now, Joni, is how you're going to cope psychologically — with your mind and your emotions I mean. When your friends all start going off to college, when they start getting lives of their own and stop visiting. You've struggled with your emotions — you've been angry, afraid... but you haven't been depressed... not yet... but that will come. Believe me, it will.'

The initial feeling of joy and relief seeped out of the room. Joni desperately clung to shreds of hope, 'I know it's going to take a long time, Doctor. You said so yourself.'

'How much time are we talking about,' Joni's dad asked.

'Are you saying that Joni isn't going to go to college this fall? We've paid a deposit for her at Maryland University — should we postpone it?' Mrs Eareckson asked quietly.

The doctor sat back on his chair and scratched his head. Raising his eyes up from the floor he looked straight at Joni and then at her parents. 'Joni isn't going to college this fall. I could tell you to postpone it... but that wouldn't be right. If you can, get your deposit back, because Joni won't be going to college this fall or next. I'm afraid that college is now out of the question for your daughter.' Looking Joni full in the face he said the words that she had been dreading, 'Joni's injury is permanent. The fusion surgery didn't sort that. I'm sorry if you didn't realise this or if we didn't explain this to you sufficiently. I thought you understood,' his voice sounded edgy, Joni's heart raced. 'Joni will never walk again.'

Joni's heart screamed, 'God, no, no, no!'

Her parent's silence didn't hide their utter shock and disbelief at this turn in events. Joni's mum turned away to face the window – a desperate attempt to hide her tears. Joni heard herself say, 'Don't worry, Mom, Dad. God wants me to walk again. I'm going to walk out of here.'

Joni's dad nodded and squeezed his daughter on the shoulder. The doctor stood up and left them to talk. But the strained atmosphere in the room meant that any real talk was impossible. Joni's parents kissed her and smiled saying that they would be back soon. Silently they both left the ward and Joni was left to her thoughts. As Joni heard their heavy tired footsteps retreating down the tiled hallway she felt like screaming out at the world, at God, at anyone who would listen, 'I just want to die! Get this over with and let me die. Don't do this to me any more!' An hour of silent torture and struggle passed as Joni fought to take on this new information. But in the middle of life shattering news, daily routines had to be seen to. A nurse came in to empty Joni's catheter bag and pass on some news. 'I've just looked out the window – you're going to have some visitors soon.'

Joni grunted in acknowledgement and then asked, 'Who?'

'Your parents,' she said as she checked the tubes and smoothed Joni's covers.

Joni sobbed, great gulping sobs and as the nurse rushed to her side with a sympathetic arm Joni explained how her parents had already been over an hour ago and that the doctor had told them to cancel college as her injury was permanent. Joni's tears fell freely as she thought about her parents crying and struggling in the car park below and their daughter crying and struggling in the ward above them.

'The doctor says that I'll never walk again.'

The nurse laid a gentle hand across Joni's face, wiping away the tear, that were quickly replaced by others.

'But he's wrong. I'm going to walk out of here,' Joni gulped. 'You'll see. I will.'

The nurse smiled, but didn't say anything. Others however did... Dick said, 'Everything works together for good.'

Joni wondered about that. 'I can't sleep at night, I'm pumped full of drugs. I can't move. I'm stuck in this frame. Dick says there's a reason for all of this – I wonder what?'

Jason, who was drifting away from God, cursed and swore at Joni and told her to fight it. 'Forget all this about it being God's will. How could God, if there is a God, let this happen to you! Fight d'y hear? Joni – fight it.'

Joni wondered about that too, 'It seems that way, Jason... but God must have some kind of reason.'

But Joni's questions weren't answered... instead more questions... and uglier ones raised their heads.

***

'Why God? Why?' Joni screamed aloud. 'How can you do this to me? What have you done?' she accused.

Joni's friend Jackie stood beside her shaking with emotion and exhaustion, a mirror clenched in her fingers, she sobbed as she saw her friend's agony and pain.

Joni hadn't realised the full extent of what the accident had done to her. In one way it wasn't just the accident, but the surgery, the drugs, the medical treatment and illness. It had all taken its toll. So much so that when two girlfriends from school had come to visit Joni – things hadn't gone at all well. Neither of them had seen Joni since her accident and when they quietly entered the ward they almost walked past Joni on her stryker frame until she called out, 'Hey there – I'm sorry I can't turn my head to see you, but if you...'

One of the girls stopped short and turned obviously shocked at the sight before her. A second's silence was quickly ended by a dull moan and a choked sob, 'Joni. Oh God no. Joni!'

Joni confused and uncertain listened to the sound of rapidly retreating steps and a deep sobbing as the girls ran out of the ward. A moment later the sound of retching in the corridor brought a nurse hurrying towards the young girls... and then there was nothing. Quiet. The swish of the swing doors and the ward was back to normal. Except Joni wasn't. For days she let the worries and thoughts fester. 'What brought that on? I didn't realise those girls were so squeamish around hospitals. Or... maybe there's another reason.'

So when Jackie came in the following day Joni told her brusquely to get a mirror.

'Uh, O.K., next time I come in. I'll bring one.'

'No. Get one now. Ask the nurse.'

'There's no rush, Joni,' she said cautiously, 'Why not wait until I can bring your own mirror from home.'

'Jackie!' Joni's tone was getting angry now.

'All right,' Jackie replied nervously getting up and moving towards the nursing station. Gingerly she held up the mirror in front of her friend and Joni screamed.

Joni's reflection was almost unrecognisable. Black teeth gaped back at her. Thin and emaciated, her eyes were dark and sunk in towards the back of her skull. A skeleton covered in yellow jaundiced skin stared back at her from the glass – not the gorgeous, vibrant seventeen year old that had beamed back at her from the mirror just months before.

Joni now knew what it was that Jackie hadn't wanted her to see and now Joni wished she hadn't seen it either.

Now she really wanted to die. 'Jackie. Please help. I can't go on like this. Help me to die peacefully. Someway that I'll feel no pain. You've got to help me. Please.'

Jackie began to sob. 'Joni, don't ask that. I can't, Joni. I just can't. I love you more than I love anyone and I don't know if that would help you or not. It kills me to see you like this. But... I can't do it. I can't.'

Joni looked at her friend's agony... and said nothing. The depression had arrived just as the doctor had said it would. And it would come back again and again in the weeks and months that stretched ahead.

Days merged into weeks and weeks into months as the mindless routine of catheters and hurried meals and Stryker frames and sleep circled round and round and round. Joni's friends were here one week and then the next the new college term had started. Dick had left too... but his loyalty to Joni meant that every weekend he made the 60 mile round trip back to visit Joni in hospital. Joni looked forward to every visit and as she heard his footfall on the ward floor there would be a sudden rush of blood to her head... and if she could have felt it ... her heart would have been beating ... anticipating his arrival, his embrace, his genuine love for her... even in this awful Stryker frame. But the end of every visit meant that again she was left, alone, with her doubts and depression. 'What if he leaves me? I can't survive without Dick. I just can't exist without him.'

What Joni didn't realise was exactly what this was costing

Dick. It was exhausting, time consuming and his studies were suffering. But his love and fierce loyalty kept him coming with encouragement, advice and a strong focus on Christ. 'Joni,' Dick said one afternoon, as he lay propped up underneath her Stryker frame, 'Listen to this. It's in James chapter 1 "When all kinds of trials and temptations crowd into your lives don't resent them as intruders but welcome them as friends. Realize that they come to test your faith and to produce in you the quality of endurance."'

Joni listened puzzled. Dick continued, 'I think this means that God means this accident to teach you something. It's like a spiritual endurance test… to see what you're made of. What do you think?'

Joni thought a little. 'Boy, have I been letting God down!'

'But the verse goes on Joni, listen. "If any of you does not know how to meet any particular problem he only has to ask God who gives generously to all men without making them feel foolish or guilty."'

Joni grinned, 'My problem is something I can't meet. We should just ask God outright to heal me! Let's do it! … Lord Jesus, I am sorry I haven't been looking to you for help but you've sent this accident to me to test my faith. Thank you for this lesson. With your help I will trust you and even this accident will work together for good. Amen.'

And as Dick disappeared down the corridor, the sound of his sneakers rubbing against the tiles, Joni prayed a prayer of sincere thanks to God for this wonderful man. She pleaded that she wouldn't lose his love, that she would be able to walk again and that everything would go back to the way that it was supposed to be for Joni, for Dick for both of them, together. She was silent for a moment, and then gently added, 'May Dick love me for me and not because of this accident.' There was no use hiding from the fact that if something didn't happen soon this relationship would be going nowhere. Neither of them wanted it to end... 'but this isn't fair on Dick,' was the nagging concern at the back of Joni's mind. 'It's not fair at all.'

Physical Therapy

Joni continued to pray that God would make everything all right – she remembered Dick's advice about how God was trying to teach her something, but Joni felt that she had learned her lesson. However, as the physical therapists came to organise her therapy sessions, Joni also remembered Jason's advice, 'You gotta fight.' Joni decided that if these classes were the way for her to get back her hands and then have her walking out of hospital – then she was going to give it everything she had.

The therapist fastened Joni's arms in slings and explained the process with some medical terminology accompanied by simple explanations and some diagrams.

'Look here, Joni, this chart shows where your fracture is. You'll have heard that it was on the fourth and fifth cervical levels. Here at the first level are the nerves for vital organs such as heart and lungs. If you have a break at that level you don't normally live. The second and third levels control our neck muscles and head movement and then the fourth and fifth levels,' she continued, 'well when you break it there – quadraplegia – as in your case – is the general result. The sixth level controls the arm muscles. Now you have some feelings in your shoulders, upper arm and chest. We're going to train other muscles in your back and shoulder to compensate for the muscles that you've lost.'

'Is that what the doctors mean about getting the use of my hands back?' Joni quizzed.

'Kind of. We've got a chart here that tells us you've got about 50 percent use of your biceps – the upper arm muscles that move the arm. But I'm afraid we're not going to know how much you'll be able to use these until you get into therapy.'

Joni nodded, 'O.K. then – Let's do it!'

And Joni began – slowly at first. Her first exercises were attempts to try and lift her arm using the muscles of her neck and shoulders. Joni had to stop trying to lift her arm in the old way but had to teach herself to use other parts of her body in new ways. Gritting her teeth she tried again and again until finally after straining all her willpower and strength, her arm rose half an inch – before flopping back limply.

The therapist exclaimed, 'Beautiful Joni! Well done!' and then 'Again,' and Joni realised that she was in for a lot of very hard work. But it would be worth it in the end – she was sure of it.

At the end of the session the therapist came over to Joni to give her a brief summing up, 'You know we've got a lot of work to do, Joni. It's going to be hard. But soon we'll have you ready for Greenoaks.'

Joni's brow furrowed in a puzzled expression. There was a word she hadn't heard before. 'Greenoaks?'

'That's the rehabilitation centre,' the therapist explained. 'The next step. It's a hospital specialising in cases like yours.'

Joni gasped, 'The rehabilitation centre! That's where I'll learn to walk!'

For weeks it was all Joni worked for and all Joni thought about. She put in one hundred and ten percent effort and at night she would dream about arriving at Greenoaks – a pleasant leafy driveway leading up to a beautiful stone building with windows and picturesque views. She would dream about the friends she would make there, the fun they would have, the hard work and the rewards as she finally stood on her own two feet and walked out of there – healed at last!

But dreams seldom measure up to reality. A shock awaited Joni when she went outside for the first time since her accident. Lying back in the stretcher she gazed up at the sky, treasuring the smell of fresh air, the tingle of sunshine on her forehead, the whisper of a breeze across her cheek. But as golden autumn colours wheeled into view Joni realised that a whole season had passed since she had come through the doors of the Emergency room. Now the smell of bonfires was in the air, not barbeques. Children ran down the street chasing leaves, scrunching them under foot and flinging them in the air. When Joni had last been outside the kids on the beach had been throwing frisbees and chasing butterflies. And then on arrival at Greenoaks there was another surprise – instead of the vision of tranquil peacefulness that she had dreamt of – there was a large grey building. No greenery or sweeping drive way, no atmospheric old building – just a sprawling low brick construction. This wasn't the only disappointment to face Joni that day. Within minutes of entering the rehab centre Joni realised that everybody there was either in Stryker frames, wheel chairs or lying in their beds staring at the ceiling. 'There's nobody cured here,' Joni wondered. 'This doesn't look good.' That last thought was quickly smothered in jumped up enthusiasm as she was wheeled into her new ward.

Four pairs of eyes swivelled to catch a glimpse of the new occupant. They were all in Stryker frames – so their line of vision was limited. But from Joni's left a cheery voice piped up, 'Hi I'm Betty – but everyone call's me BJ – that's because the other one over to your right – she's Betty too. Across the way – there's Ann and then there's Denise. What's your name?'

'Hi, I'm Joni Eareckson.'

The reaction from Ann across the room was not what Joni had expected. 'Joni Eareckson,' she drawled bitterly. 'If I hear that name again I'll puke. That's all I heard at City hospital – Joni this and Joni that.'

Joni was stunned and tried to joke it off – but eventually the atmosphere in the room thawed and the girls started filling in background details about themselves.

'Denise is here because she suffers from M.S. and Betty – she's got a broken neck like you. Ann was in City hospital, though not quite the model patient that you were as you'll have gathered from her initial conversation. She also smokes – and we wish she wouldn't.'

Joni looked across at the young girl who had, in a fit of temper, flicked her cigarette stub onto the ground. It fizzled out against the tiled rehab floors. 'Perhaps she doesn't know that that stuff causes lung cancer? It could kill you y'know,' Joni explained.

Ann looked across the room to where Joni's well meaning advice had come from – 'Bless you, child. Why do you think I'm doing it?'

Joni kept quiet after that. She knew what it was like to want to die. Ann's confusion and anger were obvious in her bitter comments and bad language. Every sentence was punctuated with swears or blasphemies. Joni made a resolution that she would try and get to know this girl better. Making friends and keeping them was incredibly important to Joni.

One afternoon Joni and B.J. were on their own in the ward — the others were away at different therapists. B.J.'s admission that she had actually been in the rehab centre for two years made Joni's initial confidence of a quick recovery seem incredibly naïve. The whole prospect of two years away from home and family was a nightmare. 'Dick is never going to be able to wait that long for me. I can't ask him to keep coming on these long haul visits from college just to spend an hour or two with his old girlfriend.'

Joni didn't think anything of using the expression 'old girlfriend' — for some time now Joni and Dick's relationship seemed to be in the process of changing into something else but Joni was still desperate to hold on to his friendship. She relied desperately on Dick — her anchor, her lifeline. There were other friends too such as Diana who had promised to call a lot more now that Joni was at Greenoaks — Jackie was having problems of her own and couldn't come as regularly as she had before. It was just another sign of how people's lives went on outside rehab — for better or worse — and Joni remained in her Stryker frame cut off from everyone. She decided to share her thoughts and concerns with B.J. that afternoon as they waited for the nurse to come round and empty their catheter bags.

'It's just that I don't want to lose them. My parents are so patient and Dick doesn't have to do these journeys but he does. I've been pretty mean to Jackie in the past — taking my bitterness out on her simply because I couldn't take it out on anyone else. I need to have my friends or I'll lose my mind,' Joni sighed.

B.J. was silent for a moment and then went, 'Too right, girl. If there's one thing I've learnt since I came in here it's keep hold of your old friends cos they're the ones that count. Don't look for sympathy from other quads or Denise or Ann over there… me neither really. You see, we're all in the same boat. We're either suffering the same as you or worse even. Don't make too many friends here is what I'm saying, Joni.'

'Why?' Joni asked, confused.

'You haven't been here long enough I suppose, but when you're staying in rehab everything is isolated and remote. It's like you're staying in some sort of ivory tower. Everyone has braces or wheelchairs or frames… it's when you go home that you come across problems. I've had people see me on the street at home and just because my legs are paralysed they think my brain's gone too. They treat you like a dummy – and then I'm just so relieved to come back here. What I'm saying is – don't be like me. I've been here two years and I've lost most of my friends from outside. This hunk of concrete is home to me now. My friends are all here. Joni – if you keep hold of your friends on the outside it's going to be a whole lot easier for you when you go back.'

And as the days went on Joni began to realise again how precious friends and family were. So many little things were done by the ones who loved Joni the most – just to make sure that she had some little comforts from home. Dad made up a little table rest – it was a typical practical gesture from the man who knew how to use his hands. It was the ideal height for Joni to rest a book or a magazine on. Now the down times on the Stryker frame weren't quite so 'down'. Reading helped to fend off the boredom of mindless day time T.V. and afternoon soaps. Jay would often come into the hospital with a copy of the latest 'Seventeen' magazine – full of colourful photo shoots of the latest fashions and celebrities. Dick, Jackie and Diana made regular visits – and didn't let Joni's accident come between them. The Stryker frame, the injuries, the depression that Joni went through so often, didn't put them off.

Dick had bought Joni a large print Bible which she could read by herself if someone turned the pages for her. On the front he wrote a message of love and support to 'My dearest Joni.' The words brought a lump to Joni's throat but now she was beginning to learn to control her emotions more. If you started blubbering when there wasn't a staff nurse nearby then you had no one to wipe your nose. Little things like that meant that Joni had to change her ways. Where she had once been ruled by her emotions she was now beginning to make small adjustments which meant she was more in control. The reality that rehabilitation was going to take more than a year had to be coped with. But even then emotions played a huge part in Joni's life... it was difficult not to let depression get the better of you. When it reared its ugly head Joni would often just give in... you could still wallow in depression without blubbering.

There was so much to cope with. Even the little things such as not being able to scratch your nose, having to rush through your meals as staff nurses had to hurry to get on to the next job. One thing that Joni had just become resigned to was her grubby matted hair. 'At least I don't have to look at it,' she thought, 'I'm sure it looks a fright. But I wish it wasn't so dandruffy. It's like a snowstorm down here when they flip my Stryker frame,' Joni grumbled to herself. However, what Joni didn't realise was that her hair was now beginning to smell. Jay's nose started to wriggle and squirm one morning when she came in to read the latest magazines with her sister. 'Gee, Joni, what is that smell?'

'Uh? Smell? What smell? I don't smell any smell?'

Jay sniffed again and came right up to Joni's head and exclaimed, 'Yuch. It's your hair Joni! When did these people last wash it? It's disgusting. It's awful it stinks so bad! I've got to do something about that!' and she promptly disappeared coming back with a basin, some shampoo and a brush and comb. Filling the basin with warm water Jay set about getting to grips with Joni's hair.

'Oh, Jay, that feels so good. I can't believe it's been over a month since they last washed my hair.'

'Nor me,' exclaimed Jay as she tweezed a couple of mats of hair and gently tugged a comb through some of the knots. 'I suppose it's just because your hair's beginning to grow back now after the operation and the drugs and all... but I still think someone should have found the time to give your hair a wash at least. There's dirt in here and matts as thick as your thumb. But that's the worst of it done... and you're smelling very fragrant, darling,' Jay smiled at her little sister who sniffed and agreed. 'Mmmm, delish!'

'Me next,' called out Denise.

'And me,' pleaded Betsy.

And soon Jay was rinsing out hair and teasing out matts from all four of the other girls in the ward – even Ann!

***

Joni was glad that Jay had washed her hair, Dick came the following evening for one of his flying visits. He looked tired and worried. Joni thought that perhaps his studies were getting him down. Joni had heard that he had lost his scholarship – she hoped that it wasn't because of all the time he was spending visiting her. Dick had explained that he had to put in more time and effort if he was to sort things out. The visits weren't going to be as frequent as they had been. Determined not to let her disappointment show Joni swallowed and sent up a quick silent prayer, 'Please be with Dick, Jesus, as he goes through this stressful time in his life. Help him with his studies… and help me to cling to you more instead of to him. I know that you are always going to be with me.'

The news that Jason was dating again brought with it mixed feelings. They had been seriously in love at one point, but that was a long time ago now. Joni was glad that he seemed to be serious about this girl he had met at college and she prayed that this would be the beginning of good things for him.

'Lord Jesus – everyone seems to be going on with their lives but I'm still stuck here. I can't move. I'm chained to this Stryker frame. I thought that I'd learned my lesson and that Greenoaks would be where I would get back my hands and learn to walk. But nothing has happened. What are you trying to tell me? Aren't you doing anything, God?'

The following morning, however, the nurse came in to discuss the new physical therapy plans that Greenoaks had devised for her. Joni realised that she had been missing this part of her life since arriving at the new building. It would be good to have another event in her day to distract her from depressing thoughts and tedium.

***

'I wish this therapy room didn't look so much like a torture chamber,' Joni whispered as she was wheeled into the purpose built room with its stretching, pulling and bending machines. The sight of some people walking with crutches and other aids made Joni remember her resolve to walk out of Greenoaks. In her mind she pictured herself making a return visit back to Central hospital to show them how wrong they had been. 'Permanent injury? Never walk again? Well just you look at me doctor! What do you say to that?' and she would do a twirl on the spot and walk off in the other direction.

But first things first and Joni had to let her body be stretched and pulled, bent and twisted in all directions. Her limp body was forced into making all sorts of stretches.

'It will keep your muscles elastic,' was the explanation.

Joni was doubtful. 'But if I can't feel these muscles anyway what does it matter if they get stiff?'

'Well – if we let that happen we'd have problems. Your blood circulation would get bad, your body would get stiff and your limbs would shrivel up – and once that happens the whole body gets twisted.' With that the therapist strapped Joni's legs to another contraption and started her on another doze of exercises.

Exercise became part of the daily routine – twenty minutes in the morning with the sole aim of getting Joni ready to use a normal bed and out of her Stryker frame. When that was accomplished it was on to the next thing and then the next... but no mention was made of when Joni would be able to walk or even use her hands.

'Next week I'm going to try and get you sitting up in a chair – it will take a bit of work – but we can do it,' an encouraging smile from Joni's therapist made Joni feel really optimistic.

'It will be good to be able to sit up. You don't know how tired I am of the same old view day in day out. In the Stryker frame it used to be either up or down – on the bed at least I get to see peoples faces when they speak to me and not their stockings… but it's still a limited view. A chair will be good!' Joni enthused.

But it wasn't as easy as it all sounded as she was soon to find out. The exercise regime was gruelling. The therapists attached her to a board which was tilted at an angle. Slowly they began to raise her from the horizontal position a few degrees at a time.

It wasn't long before Joni yelled out, 'Stop! Stop! I can't take anymore. I'm going to be sick.'

The therapist came over and patted Joni on the shoulder. 'Don't worry, it's like that for everybody first time. You see, your body has been used to lying flat. It's just adapted itself to living in that position. Now that we're trying to get you into a seated position all the blood is rushing from your head and it makes you feel as if you're going to faint. We'll keep doing this though, just a little at a time and soon your body will learn how to cope with things again. I think you'll be sitting on a chair by Thanksgiving.'

Joni smiled. It was a good date to aim for – Thanksgiving. She would really thank God if she could be sitting up in a chair in a few weeks time. And when she got her hands back and she walked out of here – that would be a day of praise! 'It's just gotta happen!' Joni urged. 'I'm not giving up.'

And then one day she was sitting up on the tilt board.

'Do you feel sick? Dizzy? Squeamish at all?'

'No,' Joni exclaimed. 'I feel fine – great in fact.'

'That's good, Joni, that's good. We'll get the doctors to come and do some tests on your muscle capability and feeling. We're going to be able to work out finally what feelings and muscle usage you do have and what you don't.'

When Diana came in that night, Joni had some encouraging news.

'I have full feelings in my head, neck and shoulders down to my collarbone. There's even a slight tingling sensation in my upper arms and chest. I can feel it just a little – like a kind of numbness – but it's definitely a feeling.'

'Wow, Joni, that's really cool. God's so good. I read this Bible verse today from John 16:24 – "I assure you that whatever you ask the Father he will give you in my name. Up to now you have asked nothing in my name; ask now and you will receive, that your joy may be overflowing."'

Joni felt a surge of anticipation. 'That's great. Perhaps God is planning something special. They're having that prayer meeting for me at church tonight.'

'What prayer meeting is that?' Diana asked.

'It's an all night prayer meeting to ask God to heal me.'

Diana gasped, 'Joni – oh wow – "ask and you shall receive" remember? Let's do it now.'

Joni's eyes shone with delight. 'Yes – I know it now – God is going to heal me. If I just keep praying and trusting.' That night Joni was almost too excited to fall asleep. She thought about the people at church praying for her all night. She added her own prayers and fought sleep. But soon it caught hold of her and her eyelids dropped, 'Maybe,' Joni yawned, 'God will have done something already when I wake up tomorrow. He could you know. I'm sure of it.'

The following morning – Joni's hopes were put on hold once again. The paralysis was still there. Nothing had changed. Under her breath Joni muttered, 'I'm trusting God and praying to him, I'm asking for healing in the name of Jesus – I just wish he'd hurry up and do something.'

Mistletoe and Memories

Joni waited with bated breath as the therapists discussed her condition. 'The bedsores have been bad but there is a considerable amount of healing and no new ones lately.'

'Yes and she's had enough sitting up time in the chair. I think she could cope with a day at home... but I'd have to insist that she comes back here for the end of visiting hours. I don't want her sleeping at home, not yet. That might open up some of these old sores and could mean Joni would be laid up for weeks.'

'I know – even a trip like this could cause problems,' Joni could hear the doubt in the therapist's voice. She screwed up her eyes willing them to let her go.

'Let me be home for Christmas! Let me be home for Christmas.'

The therapist looked across at Joni and saw the pleading in her face.

'But then a day at home would be good for her too... oh all right then, Eareckson,' she laughed. 'You're free to go – remember though like Cinderella you've got to be back here before midnight. You have a one day pass – no more.'

Joni squealed with delight. 'I'm going home,' she cried out. 'I'm going home for Christmas.'

Joni's family were overjoyed at the news and plans were made to make this a special time together – a time to put the past behind them and enjoy a good old fashioned Eareckson family Christmas. Friends from school and the Young Life group were invited round for hot chocolate by the roaring fireplace and carol singing. Joni could hardly sleep the night before she was due to go home. The dark room was extra quiet as the other girls had been allowed home for extended visits. Joni went to sleep and dreamed of last Christmas where there had been long moonlit walks in the snow with Dick, quiet moments as she strummed her guitar along to the tune of Silent Night. There had been love under the mistletoe, romance beside the warm log fire and the promise and hope of a bright, happy future. Now that future had changed. But when Joni woke up the next morning, Christmas morning, she wasn't going to wallow in a longing for the past. She left that until the presents had been unwrapped, the carols sung and the farewells said.

It hadn't been much… not even twenty four hours… but it had opened some wounds in Joni's heart that hurt her sorely. 'I didn't realise how homesick I really was until we drove up that steep avenue and pulled in at the driveway. It was the little things that hurt the most. I couldn't visit my old room even though it was just above my head. I don't know why I minded about that,' Joni sniffed as there was no one around to wipe her nose. 'I suppose it's the small familiar things that you miss so much. I really missed being able to just run outside and make snow angels. Last year we did this impromptu carol concert for the neighbours and went round all the doors.

'Then there was the whole social side of things. I just loved seeing my folks but then there was Dick and all the other youngsters from my youth group. Things have changed so much. I hated the thought that they would be looking at my legs, all useless and limp on the bed. I begged Mom to cover me up with her old travelling rug.

'I don't know,' she sighed. 'Perhaps it's like what B.J. said. Friends move on without you and if you're not careful all the friends you have end up being in here.'

The following morning it turned out that the visit home had opened up more than a few heart wounds — Joni's bed sores had opened up again, the bone protusions in her back and hips had bust them clean open.

'I'm afraid that's going to be your last visit home for a while,' the therapist grimmaced as he looked at Joni's sores in more detail. 'These aren't going to heal at all unless we get you back in a Stryker frame.'

Joni groaned.

***

Then one evening Joni watched from her Stryker frame as Dick slowly got up from the floor below her and walked away. The conversation hadn't gone well. Dick was emotionally exhausted from the accident and the gruelling journeys he had to make to come and see her. Joni could see clearly the effect it was having on her loved ones... and she did love Dick... but tonight had been the night to tell him. 'Dickie, we're holding onto the past. Things aren't going to get any better. Don't you see that?' Now she was hearing in the distance the sound of the retreating elevator. Dick had gone. She hoped he hadn't gone for good... but she couldn't make him wait any longer for her. 'It's going to be better for him... but what about me?' One tear, salty and warm trickled down her face and dropped onto the copy of the open Bible beneath her. She didn't even look at the pages. 'I can pray for some accident or miracle to kill me,' she thought desperately, 'but what is there to say that God would listen to that prayer. He hasn't listened to the others.'

The depression continued and some attempts were made at surgery to file down her bones and relieve the pressure on the skin. It might mean that the bed sores wouldn't open up again quite so easily.

After the operation there was the recovery time while the sutures and bedsores healed again. Then there was the impatient wait for physical therapy to start only to face disappointment as five minutes out of the Stryker fame Joni's incision from the operation bust right open once more. This time it would be weeks of recovery time involved. Joni was desperate.

One thought lived with her day and night as she lay in the Stryker frame trying to work out what there was left of her future.

'I just have to get the use of my hands back. I just have to... otherwise what point is there to life?'

Joni thought over the physical therapist's suggestions that she could learn to use her mouth instead of her hands. Joni was having none of it. 'It's degrading! Learning to write by holding a stick in my mouth. I'm not doing it.' Joni kind of felt that this would be an admission of defeat and she wasn't giving up. She'd said she was going to walk out of Greenoaks... well if she couldn't do that she would certainly go out of there waving. 'I'm getting my hands back. I don't care what anyone says!'

Passages of scripture from Lamentations didn't really replace the scriptures she had clung to in the past such as Psalm 23 but as her depression continued she seemed to be able to identify more with prophets like Jeremiah who had written that kind of more melancholy poetry. It was these kind of words that met her exactly where she was... in the depths of despair.

'She weeps bitterly at night,

the tears flow always on her cheeks;

no one of all her lovers now seeks to bring her comfort.

For the Lord has afflicted her

because of her great transgressions.

Look and see if there is any sorrow like my sorrow,

which is being dealt out to me,

which the Lord has inflicted in the day of his anger.

From on high he sent fire into my bones,

and it has subdued them.

He has given me over to frustration and faintness all day long.

He has made my strength to fail.

The Lord has delivered me into the hands

which I am unable to withstand.

My eyes are exhausted with weeping;

my emotions are deeply disturbed;

my grief is poured out on the earth.

Surely he has turned away from me;

He has turned his hand against me.

He has made my skin and my flesh turn old.

He has crushed my bones.

He has surrounded me with bitterness and distress.

Even when I cry aloud, I cannot go forth.

He has weighted me down with chains. He shuts out my prayer.

I have forgotten what enjoyment is.'*

* Lamentations 1:2, 5, 12-14; 2:11; 3:3-8, 17 BERKELEY)

Every word went straight to Joni's heart. Every phrase was written as she saw it, for her. Joni stayed in her depression, refusing help, turning away from the promises of God's love that would give her hope and trust. 'What's the use of believing in God when your prayers just fall on deaf ears!'

Though there were people at Greenoaks who tried to get Joni out of her depression others sent her spiralling into a deeper gloom. One of these was Mrs Barber – a blasphemous, obscene, insensitive woman who saw patients as a hindrance to be abused if at all possible. One night Joni got on the wrong side of her by answering back to some crude comment she made about Dick's photograph. As soon as the words had escaped Joni's lips a snarling face loomed above Joni's Stryker frame. 'What did you say?' she growled. 'I have to turn this Stryker frame of yours – it would serve you right if I just left it for the morning... but do you know,' the tone of her voice became more sinister and menacing, 'I think I will turn you, out of the goodness of my heart. Are you ready?' And with that she flipped Joni's Stryker frame with a violent push sending Joni spinning round the other way – Joni's loose arm ricocheted off the frame – leaving her with a huge swelling in the morning. Though she couldn't feel it – Joni knew that it was injured and Joni's mother knew this too when she saw it and eventually got the story out of the other girls in Joni's ward.

'We saw her do it, Mrs Eareckson. She just took Joni's frame and flipped ever so fast. She didn't stop to check if Joni was secure or anything and her arm just flipped out and hit the metal as she went. You can see, can't you – it's really swelling up.'

A complaint to the hospital authorities and an official

warning from the hospital supervisor didn't stop Mrs Barker's vicious behaviour.

'Just you wait,' she whispered in Joni's ear. 'If you pull a stunt like that again I'll see that you'll pay for it dearly. Do you understand me?' Then with that she was gone and Joni was left terrified.

Another resident at Greenoaks seemed, at first, to Joni, to be someone worth hanging out with, listening to and discussing things with. Jim was going through so many of the same questions and problems and issues that Joni was tackling. His conclusion was that there was no God, and that the only meaning you could get out of life was what you brought to it yourself.

His viewpoints confused Joni for a while, she even got deeply into some of the literature he suggested. Many hours were spent reading books by Sartre, Marx and Kafka – books that, instead of answering her questions, just confused Joni more and did nothing to deal with her depression.

As she lay awake one night, her mind restlessly flitting over questions and problems she asked herself why it was that she had devoted so much of herself to these books and pamphlets that had pointed her away from God.

'I know I've been asking if God's turned his back on me... I've even been questioning if he existed. But this whole thing about living for the moment, getting what you can out of life now... it just doesn't ring true for me. Jim thinks I'm foolish to be preparing for heaven. After you're dead... you're dead... or that's what he says. But I learnt in High school that there's nothing in life that satisfies me. Getting what I can out of life for me doesn't bring lasting fulfilment. There has to be something permanent. But then this accident's made me question everything. Is there any purpose to it? I've kept asking that question… and if God were real surely he would show me?'

Joni pondered some more. Bringing to mind Jim's arguments, the books, Bible verses, well meant advice. She finally came to a crossroads. 'I know that there are only two decisions. God either exists or he doesn't. If he doesn't exist then I can't see any real reason for going on living. What can I do? I want to believe but I've nothing to hang onto. God, prove you exist! I need proof!'

Exhausted and confused, tired and drifting on a sea of bewildering thoughts and arguments, a verse floated into her memory, soothing her troubled mind. *'You will keep him in perfect peace, whose mind is stayed on you.'* Moments later Joni was asleep, deep peaceful breaths, a quiet untroubled mind.

The following morning she woke up refreshed. It wasn't just a new day, it was a new start. The old doubts had gone. She still had questions but she knew who to turn to… and even those questions that weren't being answered quite in the way she had hoped – these didn't throw her into the despair that they had in the past.

Old scriptures seemed to zone right into Joni's problem spiritual areas. *'My thoughts are not your thoughts neither are my ways your ways.'* It wasn't exactly an answer to her question, 'Why am I paralysed? Why are you doing this to me?' – at least not the answer Joni had been waiting for. But it was an answer – it told her to wait. Joni knew that the great God of eternity was working on a different schedule… and that wasn't necessarily Joni's schedule.

While confiding in Diana that afternoon Joni told her friend about her troubles and depression and how God had brought her through it. 'I suppose when I'm lying here in this frame day in day out – a year can feel like a century. But in God's eyes a thousand years can be like a day in his perfect plan. It's quite something to get used to.'

'Joni, you're so right. I'm glad you're looking at things this way. It's a real turning point for you. You don't have to know why God let you be hurt... but you do know this... he knows that you are hurt. That's all that counts. Trust him, Joni, to work it all out. He will eventually work out all things for good. If not right now... one day... for all of us.'

Joni smiled, 'for all of us'... that included Jason and his new girlfriend, Dick and the choices he would have to make in his life, Jay who was struggling with divorce papers and the prospect of being a single mom, Joni's parents who were coming to terms with the fact that their little girl who was once so active would never walk again and Joni – who was struggling and learning and beginning to move on.

'Oh, and I've something to tell you,' Diana ducked back under the Stryker frame with a great big grin on her face. 'I've chucked in school. I'm going to spend a year in prayer and meditation waiting on God to tell me what he wants me to do with my life. And to keep me out of mischief, I'm going to become a volunteer at Greenoaks.'

And with a wave and a cheeky grin Diana disappeared out the door.

'So that's why she was wearing those overalls!' Joni gasped.

***

Having Diana at Greenoaks was great. Joni loved it and Diana did too. She still spent time with Joni but she also followed the other rehab staff – shadowing them and finding out how they did things, learning to help where she was needed... and one of the places she was most needed was beside Joni's Stryker frame, sharing news, giving advice and listening. One conversation had been long and very difficult for Joni. It all surrounded the thought of 'What's next for Joni.'

'I don't know what will happen when I go home,' Joni mumbled doubtfully. 'Jay's asked me to come stay with her and little Kay, she's Jay's daughter you know. Well, it's something I've been thinking about... but I just don't know if it's the right choice. What is going to happen to me? It could be months maybe years before I get my hands back. What am I supposed to do?' Joni looked questioningly into Diana's eyes. Diana sat there quietly, thinking.

'You don't know what you're supposed to do. There's therapy for a start. You've been avoiding it. I know it seems pointless to you – this whole stick in mouth business – but if God knows the purpose and meaning of things he can give meaning to your life too – paralysed or not. But Joni I've got to say it – you've been fighting him on this one.'

Joni acknowledged this with a brusque sniff before Diana went on. 'What if you never get back the use of your hands?'

That question left Joni reeling. 'God wouldn't leave me like this for ever would he?' she wondered. But as Joni had admitted before – she didn't know what God's plan was for her... so perhaps ...

The following morning Joni had a meeting with her occupational therapist and she was booked in for some sessions.

'First we're going to teach you how to write. Hold this pencil in your mouth like that... yes that's right. Not so tight though. That's better.'

Then with some mumbling acknowledgments and

some stumbling attempts Joni eventually learned enough, after many hours of practice, to be able to write a letter home to her parents.

The following months meant further operations... but this time they were successful. Other changes happened for the better too. Joni's choice of books improved. Diana was pleased to see copies of C. S. Lewis and other well known Christian writers propped up on Joni's little reading shelf beneath her Stryker frame. And then things began to look brighter as Joni's therapists discussed getting her to use a wheelchair and even trying her hand – or mouth – at some art. At first she was a bit doubtful about this. Her stumbling awkward attempts at painting tiles were nothing like the fabulous pictures she had been praised for before her accident. But as she looked at her progression she began to see a definite improvement.

'Let me see Joni,' Joni's art therapist leaned over the clay slab that Joni had just etched in and gasped, 'That's really good. I'm impressed. We should have had you doing this earlier.'

Joni smiled and looked with a critical eye over the simple sketch she had just done. A cowboy on a horse. How many times had she seen that very picture as she had gone on treks with her sisters or watched her father riding over the ranch as the sun sunk below the distant mountains.

'The talent's in the mind Joni. The hands are just a tool. You're an artist – your eye sees, you understand. That skill hasn't disappeared.' Joni could see that the therapist was right. And as she looked at the picture she had just drawn – the line of the horse's back, the angle of the stetson, the memories came flooding back of bareback riding, glorious sunsets, deep mountain valleys and meadows saturated with wild flowers... colour explosions, subtle tinges from the brush of the great artist himself – God. Joni flushed with the intense joy of discovering creativity again. It was a gift from God and she was so thankful.

Praise The Lord

Things were improving spiritually too. Joni still had questions, the old questions, but she began to add others. 'How can I glorify God? What can I do with my life?' And even though nothing was really making any sense – Joni knew that God knew and that he understood and that was all that mattered in the end.

As she listened more to her friends and their problems, to the staff in the hospital, to her sister and her family... Joni realised that instead of being in a uniquely awful position she was actually more like the people around her than she had at first realised. They all had problems too. People went round and round with their jobs and their lives, the nine to five, the fight for life. But one thing that Joni hadn't realised up till now was that where she had been brought face to face with how 'meaningless' life could really be... most of the people outside her Stryker frame didn't know that a life without Christ was 'meaningless'.

'God taught me that through this accident. I suppose that's one of the lessons he meant me to learn... I may have others. Before my life was full of parties and shopping and meaningless conversations. I let these things get in the way of what really mattered – God. Now my life is just whittled down to the basics – eating, sleeping, breathing.'

And even as she identified more with the people around her she began to realise that there was someone else she could add to that list... Jesus Christ.

'I never thought about it before I suppose, not really. Not in this way... but Jesus Christ was paralysed too when he was on the cross.' Joni's mother looked into her daughter's eyes and nodded.

'Your right honey. He understands your suffering even better than you do yourself... it's the same with so many things. He cares and he knows.'

And as Joni thought about the nails that went through her Lord's hands and feet, about the excruciating pain of being fixed to the cross waiting for death – hopeless and helpless – she appreciated him more and what he had done for her. The old truths of Young Life meetings and summer camps came flooding back... That's why Jesus came... that's why he had to die... he died because of my sin... he took the punishment.

The verses that had spoken to Joni in the book of Lamentations in previous weeks still spoke to her but in a different way as she listened to other scriptures that Diana read out to her in her spare time. Some verses read as though they had been written just for her – a young woman, hurt and alone but struggling to find out how to best please God in her life. Psalm 41:3 for example 'The Lord will sustain me on my sickbed.' Written hundreds of years before Stryker frames and hospital wards even existed Joni could still see that that verse was meant for her in 1968.

***

'What's that, Joni?' the art therapist asked one morning as he leaned over the easel that Joni was working on.

'Mmmbbf?' Joni mumbled the question before flicking the brush out of her mouth. 'What did you say?'

'That mark you've put in the corner of the picture?'

Joni squinted to see what she'd put there and then smiled. 'It's my new signature – P.T.L. – stands for Praise the Lord and that's what I'm doing now.'

And that's what she was doing when days later she heard that not only was she going home for Christmas but that there might be an opening for her at Rancho Los Amigos in Los Angeles.

'That's the place where they send the "impossible cases" isn't it?' Joni's face shone in anticipation. 'That's where I'll get back the use of my hands.'

Joni heard the news about her acceptance into Rancho Los Amigos over the Christmas holidays. Greenoaks was now in the past… the future was Los Angeles… 'That's where I'll get back the use of my hands!'

***

'Would all the remaining passengers for United Airlines Flight 347 to Los Angeles, California, please make their way to the boarding gate as their flight is about to depart.'

Joni listened with mounting excitement to the efficient voice of the airport clerk that crackled over the tannoy system. Joni was already being wheeled in a stretcher down the adjoining passageway and was soon being expertly lifted by Greenoaks staff into one of the reclining chairs. Again there were instructions about flight procedures and how to cope with a paraplegic passenger but Joni had been through this procedure in cars and with family so many times before it was hardly worth noticing… but the aeroplane, the flight, this was all new and exciting. The air hostesses in their stylish suits and petite hats perched on perfectly styled hair. The tickets, the passenger safety cards, the take off, the food trolleys going up and down the aisles with snacks and drinks – everything was a new experience to Joni – a thrill after having been cooped up for so long with only short visits home to break up the monotony.

As the plane began its ascent into the clouds Joni dreamed of the hopes and plans for her future. Old wishes resurfaced again as she held on to the hope that God's will for her was to get her hands back.

'Once my hands are back there won't be anything to stop me getting married to Dick. I'll be able to live a normal life, get married, keep house – be useful, lead a meaningful, normal life. I can see God's plan for good actually happening now. This is what he has meant for me all along. He was never going to leave me helpless.'

Over 3,000 miles later the plane began its descent into Los Angeles airport. Joni could feel the balmy warmth as they made their way through the corridors to the baggage reclaim. Outside a heat haze flickered off the tarmac and another jet engine roared into life as it lifted off the runway and headed for the sky.

Joni now looked forward to another new experience… but having learned her lesson at Greenoaks, this time she didn't build up any mental pictures of what Rancho Los Amigos would look like. However, Joni was pleasantly surprised. 'The building's beautiful!' But it wasn't just the exterior that impressed Joni – inside was excellently kitted out too. 'They are well staffed here,' Joni pointed out to Jay who had come down to Los Angeles to be with her sister, renting an apartment not far away from Rancho. 'You can tell by the way the staff treat you that they're happy here.'

Jay nodded, 'You're right. The working conditions are better than Greenoaks and I've heard that the pay is too.'

Joni grinned, 'If I tell Diana do you think she'll leave her job at Greenoaks and come work here?'

Jay smiled. One week later – there was a surprise for Joni. 'Ta da!' Diana exploded into the ward with a deep theatrical bow – almost sending Joni into hysterics with astonishment – for beside her were two other dearly loved friends – Jackie and Dick.

'I don't believe you guys! How did you do it? What are you doing here? Diana? Jackie? Dick! Come over here and explain yourselves.'

Laughing and joking the three friends sprawled themselves out on chairs, or across Joni's bed and immediately went into the long exciting recount of their mammoth, non stop, car journey from Maryland to Los Angeles.

'We got so lonesome, Joni. We just had to come and see you. It's just not the same without our favourite girl. But I can see this place is good. It's really professional,' Diana looked around a bit obviously comparing Rancho to Greenoaks. 'When do you start therapy?'

'They've started already.'

'Already. That's quick. What are you doing?'

'Well I'm getting on really well – they strap my arms with braces and try to train my shoulders and back muscles to raise my arms. I've got all these other muscles that I haven't really been using that much before the accident. This therapy is training me to use them to do the things that the paralysed muscles used to do. I can raise and lower my arm to a certain extent but there's no finger movement. I can't bend my wrist or do any grasping.'

'So what are they training you to do exactly?' Jackie asked puzzled.

'Well, I'm being taught to feed myself.'

'You're kidding me, Joni! That's great!' Dick exclaimed. 'But I thought you said you couldn't grasp? How are they getting you to hold a spoon or fork?'

'Well they've made me my own special spoon – bent at a precise 45 degree angle – this is deftly attached to my arm brace by which I will soon be able to scoop a whole bite of mashed potatoes and insert into my mouth, chew and swallow as per normal,' Joni smiled, then added, 'I know it's not much but when you've been waiting as long as I have been… you feel it's a great achievement… or at least it will be when I can do it.'

'Of course it will be, Joni! It's huge. It's awesome!' Dick exclaimed.

'Too right,' Diana added. 'I'm impressed with these guys. They really know how to work. You'll be out of here in no time.'

'Uh, I know. April 15th to be precise.'

At which all three friends gasped in astonishment.

'That's three months, Joni?'

'I know. I didn't think it would take so little time to get my hands back either.' Joni smiled across at Dick who smiled back. Perhaps they did have a future together after all.

***

Joni's therapy sessions continued and soon she was actually eating the mashed potatoes by herself. Then it wasn't long before she was using a wheelchair – having whacky races with other residents down the corridor and getting a ban on her electric wheelchair and a speed limit as punishment for some particularly crazy wheel spins. Joni loved the opportunity the wheelchair gave her for some independence and often she would nip out onto the Californian streets and drive to one of the near by fast food outlets to pick up some fries or a taco or perhaps a burger for some of the less mobile Rancho residents.

'It's amazing how they really cater for wheelchair users here,' Joni pointed out one day to Diana. 'Just look at the pavements – even the curbs are sloped gently for easy wheelchair use. I can get all the way up to the counter at the Taco Bell and I only have to ask for help to get my money out. The guy at the Taco Bell is neat – he reckons I should enter my chair into the speed car rally.'

Dick jumped in to their conversation – 'Reckon he's right there. But you've still got that ban – so go easy, tiger!'

'Hmm O.K. then boss!' Joni quipped. 'But I can't believe you guys are going off already. Three weeks has passed so quickly.'

'I know, Joni – and we've loved it. Staying at Jay's was great and being able to see you everyday.'

'I know. I really appreciated what you guys did – coming all this way. I really love you.'

Joni said it to all three of her friends, but her eyes stayed longer on Dick's face and he smiled and kissed her. 'You just focus on all that therapy you've got to do and get out of here. We'll be seeing you soon!'

With their baggage already piled up in the back of the car all the friends had to do now was say their goodbyes, give hugs and kisses and then they were away... the sound of the hooting horn blaring out as they disappeared round the corner.

Joni went back into Rancho with new resolve to work as hard as she could until April 15th – and surely by then she would have her hands back. Week by week she worked and slogged, training muscles, learning new skills. It was tiring, exhausting, work – but Joni was determined. And then the big day came – April 15th. Joni's doctor walked smartly into the room with a smile on his face. 'Well Joni – you've made it. Congratulations. All that hard work has really paid off. You've reached all your rehabilitation goals and you're ready to go home.'

'All my goals?' Joni wasn't so sure about that. 'Ready to go home?' She had come to Rancho Los Amigos to get back the use of her hands. That hadn't happened. Some straight talking was needed here.

'I've been working hard, doctor – but I've been working to get back the use of my hands... now I'm wondering if I ever will.'

Looking Joni straight in the eye the doctor's reply was blunt. 'You are never going to get back the use of your hands, Joni. Give up on the idea and get used to it.'

That evening as Joni supervised Jay's packing of her clothes and belongings Joni also took some time to write a difficult but much needed letter.

'*Dear Dickie,*

For some reason God has chosen not to answer our prayers. I will never be able to use my hands. That means I will always be dependant and helpless. I can never be a wife. I know you love me, as I do you, yet God must have some other plan for both of us. Let's remain friends but I want you to be free to choose other relationships. Date other girls and look for God to lead you to the woman you are supposed to marry. I can never be that woman. Joni.'

With Rancho Los Amigos behind her Joni's last hope for rehabilitation was behind her. She had hoped for so much and had achieved it but she had still failed on what she had ultimately set out to do – get back her hands.

'I'm going to be like this as long as I live!' The awful realisation was hard to cope with and even as she made the journey home Joni spiralled into a deeper depression than she had ever been in.

'I just don't get it, Dad,' Joni complained one morning. 'Why me? Is God punishing me? I look at this house, all the things that you've made. You've left us this great legacy. What will I leave behind? Nothing! My hands are useless I can't make anything significant. I'm dependant on people to do the most basic things for me.'

'This morning Mom had to wash me and feed me, Jay had to brush my hair and tie my buttons. When I want to wipe my nose someone has to do that for me. I can't even hug you – though right now I want to.'

Joni's dad looked lovingly into his daughter's face.

'Sweetheart. Maybe we'll never know why you are suffering, but I know one thing, God knows what he is doing. So many times I've been in church and listened to people's pious prayers about how they're wicked sinners undeserving of God's goodness. They thank Jesus for saving them with one breath and then with the other they complain about suffering and trouble. If we really believe that we deserve only the worst – hell – and then we only get a taste of it when suffering comes along – well I reckon we should try and live with it somehow... don't you?'

'But what if God is punishing me?'

'Joni – don't dwell on that. You know, honey that Jesus has dealt with all that at the cross. Like I said, we don't know why he's let this happen to you... but we have to believe that he knows what he's doing.'

Joni sighed. 'I suppose,' she muttered half-heartedly. But at the core of her heart resentment festered. 'God's really let me down,' Joni bitterly complained. 'This is what betrayal feels like!'

As a result of this bitter anger against God Joni deliberately went out of her way to displease him. Shutting him out of her world – she shut everyone else out too and lived her life through fantasies and memories of past experiences.

It started with remembering sensations that she had lost that day on Chesapeake Bay.

'Cool fresh water, slipping over my skin. I come up from out of the surf – droplets are clinging to my body and my bathing suit. The sun is baking hot – my skin is tingling. I reach up and run a hand through my hair. The sand scratches between my toes.

'I smell the aroma of the stables. Tumbleweed is whinnying – she is pleased to see me. Striding over to her stable I saddle her up and mount. We trot briskly through the yard out into the meadow. Beneath my thighs I feel her strength and energy – with a squeeze I urge her into a canter, from a canter into a gallop. Soon we are thundering over the fields, through forests, along trails. The wind is in my hair. I can feel the thump of my heart.'

These dreams though innocent in themselves were selfish rebellion against God and they progressed to dreams and fantasies that were much more serious. Instead of riding out alone with Tumbleweed Joni's dreams brought in Jason – where together they would ride out through the woods, enjoying long treks, exhilarating gallops, sunsets and passion. Feelings that Joni had felt before and shouldn't have rose again in her heart and mind – just as sinful even though they were only thoughts. Joni's naps and daydreams were shutting out reality and were not healthy for her in any way. When Diana came to stay for the summer Joni's strange behaviour was one of the first things she noticed.

'Joni? Joni?'

Joni was flat on her back. The sun on her face brought back memories of summer walks with Jason. Right now she was there – in his arms, the warm breeze, the touch of his lips.

Diana came right up to Joni's face and yelled, 'Joni! Are you ill? What's wrong?'

Befuddled and confused Joni came too – it was a bit of a shock to come back to reality so suddenly. When she saw Diana standing there accusingly she just grunted. 'Leave me alone! Just leave me alone!'

'No I won't!' Diana retorted angrily. 'Don't think I don't know what you're doing. All this escaping from reality isn't helping one bit Joni! Face the truth – leave the past behind. It's the past that's dead – not you!'

'Oh yeah?' Joni asked sarcastically. 'Is that right? Diana, look at me. I have nothing – nothing to live for anymore. Everything has been taken away from me. What kind of life do I have really? This isn't living. I have nothing!'

'Nothing? Nothing? Go back to Greenoaks! Go back to Rancho – there were people there who really did have nothing! Were you so self absorbed that you didn't see the guy with his eyes blown out? What about the woman who couldn't speak? Joni – come on – there were people there who had lost their minds. You've got your eyes, your ears, the power of speech – your intellect! Do you call that nothing? I don't!'

And as the days passed and Joni's fantasies got more involved she realised that they were in fact taking control of her life. They weren't helping and neither was Joni's rebellious temper tantrums against God. 'I used to think that sin was just the things you did that were against God. Now that I'm paralysed I don't have the opportunities to do these sins anymore but I still think them.'

Joni gazed at the scripture passage she had just read. The scriptures told her what she was supposed to do and not to do. But she had been deliberately disobeying God through her thoughts... not her deeds... but in her paralysed state Joni knew for the first time that her thought life was as big a part of her existence before God as her physical life had once been.

'Sin is part of my nature. It's key to my make up.'

This was a solemn thought.

'I prayed once before for God to change me to do something in my life and look where it got me. I still don't know why he let this happen... but as Daddy says... we have to believe that he knows what he's doing. I think the time has come for another one of those prayers,' Joni admitted to herself.

'Lord, I know you must have something planned. Please help me to understand your will. Do something in my life to help serve you. Amen.'

The Summer of '69

'I don't know, Diana. I look over the last two years and I don't like what I see. I'm not talking about the accident as such or my paralysis – more my spiritual state. The way I've been with God. There have been emotional highs and lows – mostly lows... but there have been spiritual highs and lows – definitely mostly lows.'

'You're not on your own there, Joni. Lots of us go hot and cold with God – no one's spiritual life is what it should be... certainly not mine... but what you've been saying has started me thinking. There's this young guy you should meet. I've met him through the Young Life groups, Bible studies and other church meetings. He's different. A really strong Christian. I've had this feeling for a while now that he'd be a really good guy for all of us to get to know better. Dick, Jay, you – all of us.'

'What is it about this guy?'

'Well his name is Steve Estes and I suppose it's just his amazing spiritual maturity. Incredible for a guy so young.'

'Exactly how old are we talking about here?'

'Sixteen.'

'Sixteen!' Joni exclaimed. 'Why he's still in high school! Are you sure? He's a kid!'

'Come on, Joni – you're the one who always says you don't like it when people judge you because of your chair. Don't judge him because of his age. Meet the guy first – then make an opinion. It's only fair.'

Joni reluctantly agreed and Diana organised a visit.

It would be the beginning of months and years of Bible study and get togethers where the young people learned about God and each other.

***

Many months later Joni was sitting alongside Diana, Jay and Steve at one of their regular Wednesday night Bible studies and Joni couldn't believe how much she had learned. She shared this with the group.

'For years – even before my accident when things were going well in my life then things were going well with God… but as soon as a problem arose or a disappointment – then things just crashed around me and my spiritual life came crashing down too. What these studies have given me is a real appreciation of the basics of Christianity. I have a better understanding now of sin, salvation and putting God's word into practice.'

Steve nodded as Joni continued, 'Simple things like how to deal with sin. I didn't realise what the Bible was teaching me about it to resist and to flee. If I'd known that before and practiced it what a difference that would have made to my life. These Bible studies, Steve, have helped me so much. You'll never know how much. You've shared your wisdom with us, God's word has been explained to me. I've never really experienced this before. That first day that I met you when you came into this room and told me of how powerfully God was working in the lives of people you knew. Why that just blew me away. Before that I'd been spiralling into one of the worst cases of depression that I'd ever experienced… God gave you the right words to say to me then. It was what I needed to hear.'

'Thank you, Joni. I'm glad that God has used me to help

in this way... that he's opened up his word and used his Holy Spirit to reach out to you. It's God's Holy Spirit who has been your real instructor though. Throughout all this it has been he who has been working in all of our hearts.'

'Yeah, Joni,' Diana joined. 'Who would have thought that you would come so far as you have done in these last few months.'

'We're proud of you,' Jay added squeezing Joni on the shoulder.

Joni blushed. 'Putting the past behind me was difficult. Selling Tumbleweed was perhaps one of the hardest things... but having her standing there in the stables, whinnying in the paddock... it was only a reminder of what I didn't have. I've got rid of the temptations which made me fantasise about my past and I've focused on the future... whatever that might hold.'

'Who knows?' Jay smiled. 'You're a college graduate now, in public speaking no less.'

Joni laughed, 'How I needed that course. Do you remember Steve?'

Steve grinned, 'Yeah I remember. You sat in front of a crowd of about twenty teenagers just about to give your testimony. I was sure you were going to pass out on me or something. But despite it all you didn't do too badly. Every one is nervous on their first time at speaking in public.'

'It was about that time that my fantasies ended. I haven't given into them since. One of the Bible studies played a big part in that. Do you remember that conversation we had about heaven?'

'Yeah,' Steve nodded. 'We talked about the reality of what is waiting for God's people. That there is going to be a day, Joni, that you will no longer be paralysed. On the glorious resurrection day you will be given a new body that can walk, run, dance, do everything and more.'

Joni nodded and let her heart and mind savour the reality of that sure and certain hope. 'It was then that I realised the real meaning of that verse where we are told to *"Set our hearts on things above not on earthly things that will not last."* So many scriptures have spoken to me in new ways this last year. *"Endure life with patience,"* is one I've turned to again and again… and I'm sure you have too. I know that coping with me isn't easy at the best of times.'

Joni's friends laughed. 'It's like you said, Joni,' Jay smiled at her sister. 'You look on your wheelchair as a tool now and not a tragedy. We do too. I'm sure we wouldn't have done half the things we've done this year if it weren't for you. We're even part of a singing group now with plans for our first concert in a couple of months time. Joni – you've been a real task master – drilling us on our scales!'

'Yeah! I can see us all now on the big night! Taking our bows in front of a cheering audience throwing flowers and bouquets…' Diana stood up and gave one of her theatrical bows, to the right and then to the left.

'Steady on, Diana. It's only a church social we're going to – not the Carnegie Hall,' Steve laughed. 'But you've got one of these Young Life meetings next week Joni haven't you?'

'Yeah. I was at one yesterday for girls at the local school.'

'Really how did that go?' Diana asked intrigued.

'Quite well I think. They were asking a lot of difficult questions, you know, about my faith, why I think God has let this happen to me. The usual questions about sex and how come I'm so old fashioned as to believe that sex outside marriage is wrong. I just had to be honest and tell them that from my own experience I knew that it was. I told them again that it was one of those sins that you had to flee from and not flirt with. I've just seen so much guilt and remorse over this particular sin – it destroys otherwise happy lives and successful marriages. But I know that with God's help we can repent and put it behind us. God separates our sin from us forever because of what his Son has done on the cross. Another basic that these Bible studies have taught me. I'm telling you 1969 was a good year!'

Jay nodded, 'But 1970's brought it's own heartaches.'

With this comment Joni sighed.

'What's the news on your sister Linda?' Steve asked concerned. For Joni and Jay's five year old niece Kelly had been diagnosed with cancer and in February 1970 had passed away. 'We were all told to expect the worse,' Jay's voice caught in a sob, 'but with Linda's husband leaving her, she's on her own bringing up the other children. It's just so hard on her.'

'But seeing her little girl Kelly's own spiritual development during that time was amazing. She was a real example to us all,' Joni whispered quietly. 'I still ask questions about why it had to be her and not some other person. Hasn't our family gone through enough? Why did God let this happen to someone so young? But I have learned that there is nothing but unhappiness in trying to second guess God's purposes. We're not always responsible for our circumstances but we are responsible for how we react to them. I can feel this tragedy bringing our family closer together… closer to Jesus.'

Steve reached out for his Bible and flicked it open to Philippians 1:12. 'Look Joni, I've been meaning to share this verse with you. To close up our Bible study tonight I think I'll read it. I believe that this verse has a real message for you.

"I want you to know my brothers that what has happened to me has, in effect, turned out to the advantage of the gospel."

'I firmly believe that in the light of all that you and the others have been saying tonight what happened to you at Chesapeake Bay has turned out to the advantage of the gospel. God has perhaps even greater plans in store for you. But what he has already accomplished through you and your wheelchair has meant that tonight we've talked about deep spiritual truths, a family brought close through tragedy, young women have been told to flee from sin. Joni – God is working through you. Your paralysis could even be a blessing.'

'Hmm... well I don't know about that,' Joni thought out loud. 'I don't think I'm there with you yet, Steve.'

'But you might be... one day. We've all still got some way to go yet.'

***

'Steve was right you know,' Joni said to Diana the following week.

'About what?'

'About having some way to go yet. I mean – I've realised that there are still one or two things that I have problems with. Probably more... but two things came to light this week. Lately I've been struggling with being thankful. I don't know, the feeling I guess just wasn't there. I knew all the things I had to be thankful for – my salvation, forgiveness, my family, my voice, so much.'

Diana smiled, 'I remember a day... was it only last summer... when I was yellin' and screamin' at you about just those very things?'

Joni laughed, 'Yeah and I deserved everything I got. But

in the middle of all this struggle I just decided that I would thank God anyway... even though I didn't feel like it. And over the last few days I've begun what I suppose I could describe as a thankful habit. But this morning as I began my habit of thanks... something was different. I actually felt thankful. The feeling was back!'

'And there's something else I've learned. Steve was talking about how I'm always putting myself down, being negative, on the defensive... you know?'

'Uh huh, Joni, I know!'

'Really? – Well we were talking about it and he reckoned that I was too hung up on my self image... that I care too much about what people think. And he's right – I keep comparing myself to others. Oh, I even feel depressed about my looks when I see a mannequin!'

'Oh Joni!'

'I know. Stupid eh?'

'There you go again... you're not you know.'

'I know. Steve was saying that this is what happens when we let society determine our values.'

'What does he mean by that?' Diana asked.

'Well, if I care about what others think about the way I look, the way I dress, I'm fighting a losing battle. What matters is what God thinks. His values are the only ones that are important. I remember something that my Dad said to me once. What is important is the character we build. That's our legacy – the only one that counts.'

'Gee, Joni,' Diana exclaimed, 'I reckon that's a lesson I really need to learn too. Not just you.'

Right then Jay popped her head round the door. 'But you do know, Joni, that just because you're working on your character and not giving a fig about what the world thinks of your looks or fashions… doesn't mean you have to give up on make-up entirely. With your hair back in condition and your skin looking so much better – would you like Diana and me to give you a mini-makeover? We could go shopping tomorrow too. We could kit you out in some clothes that fit you for a change.'

Joni's eyes lit up. 'Let's do it!'

***

'I can't believe that Steve's left already.' Joni sighed one morning in the fall. The burnished leaves, all crisp and golden, were dropping, bit by bit, from the trees outside the Eareckson home. Jay had popped in for a coffee and a chat.

'Steve's gone to college?' Jay was surprised. 'Where has the summer gone? All the kids are off to college. The old oak by the cottage is ablaze with copper and gold. I look out on it every morning. Its something you'd love to paint, Joni.'

'Hmm. I like the sound of that. But there's a real nip in the air. I don't think I could stay out long enough to paint it properly. I'd want to do it justice,' Joni mused.

'I was kind of thinking that there might be room at the cottage for you to stay a while… maybe for keeps. You could set up a studio in one of the back rooms – I hope you don't mind but I've spoken to Mum and Dad about it. Dad's even thinking about building an extra wing. You know what he's like – give him a hammer and give him a spade. There's no stopping him.'

Joni looked at Jay astonished. 'Are you sure?'

'I told you before you left Rancho that I wanted you to come and stay with me and Kay. Your little niece would just love to have her auntie to come live with her. Now seems like a good time. We got on well at that Young Life camp in the summer when we went to help out on the leadership team. I don't think we should have any fears that we'd fall out or anything.'

'Fall out? Of course not. You're so patient, Jay. You're always cleaning up after my friends and helping me when it's obviously inconvenient for you. I'd love to stay with you. And I promise that I'll tell my friends to wash their own dishes – is that agreed?'

'Agreed,' Jay smiled broadly and kissed her little sister on the forehead. 'You're sweet and I love you and we're going to have a great time – single girls together.'

And Joni laughed... but even though she laughed, singleness, marriage – or the lack of it – was something that often bothered Joni.

That summer had brought the usual wedding celebrations and bridal showers. It was hard for Joni when she sang at the weddings, dressed in bridesmaid's dresses and even on occasion caught the bridal bouquet. As well as Kathy and Butch getting married, school friends, people from church – were either dating, engaged or planning a wedding in the very near future.

'I thought I'd got over all this,' Joni accused herself as she left yet another friend's wedding with the old feelings of frustration and resentment fighting their way to the fore.

'Lord, I know that I am content as I am... but I suppose I will always wonder if you've got a man for me?' However, when Joni began asking God these questions on a more regular basis something happened. Joni met someone... Donald.

'It was at the Young Life meeting. That's where I met him,' Joni gushed. 'He works with disadvantaged kids and his project's supported by our church.'

Jay listened patiently, but her questions and doubts were written clearly on her face. Joni continued regardless. 'He's goodlooking, intelligent, committed and he wants to see me again. But as for him turning up at the door unannounced like that this morning,' Joni blushed. 'Sorry about that. It wasn't quite what I was expecting. But he was so relaxed... didn't you think?'

'Yup. He was definitely relaxed. So relaxed he stayed for lunch, got relaxed some more and stayed for dinner. What did you guys find to talk about all that time?'

'Oh, this and that,' Joni said vaguely. 'It was nice of him to offer to drive me to college. But seeing as you know my needs and my routine – it would have been too much for him.'

'Of course... especially on a first date.'

Joni laughed.

But the following day after college was finished Donald was outside waiting for Joni and Jay as they exited through the gates. 'Great to see you, Joni. How about a coffee?' and that was the beginning.

Joni and Donald's relationship gradually progressed. Longings and desires that she had felt were long buried soon resurfaced. Joni loved Donald's spontaneity. The way he didn't just sit back and accept things. You never heard him say – that can't be done. He had to try it first, and try it again – before he would admit defeat. He did mad and crazy things like pushing Joni in her wheelchair into the middle of the surf. Pounding waves crashed around them – but Joni was secure in Donald's strong athletic arms. The excitement was thrilling and, although she couldn't feel it, Joni knew that her heart was pounding. The danger of the waves and the passion she felt for Donald – it had lit something deep inside her.

Donald's determination triggered off other emotions too. He refused to accept that it was God's will that Joni remain in a wheelchair for the rest of her life and he began to persuade Joni that she should be praying for healing, even attending meetings where miracles were promised – 'if you only believed'.

Joni listened to Donald's enthusiasm. He was saying what she had longed to hear... and now she too believed that God planned to heal her. They even discussed marriage and what that would mean.

Joni began to believe not just that she might be healed but that Donald might be the man that God had planned for her to marry. He could defintely cope with her disability. Nothing seemed a problem to him.

'It's wonderful,' Joni thought as she was pulled into Donald's arms for a long lingering kiss. 'God has given me this magnificent man just at the time I needed him. Diana is getting married soon and off to make a family of her own. God knows my every need. This is his plan for me. It's so exciting.'

Joni shared these thrilling emotions with her sister who sounded a note of caution. 'Joni, I don't want to see you hurt or disappointed. Please be careful. Just be careful.'

But Joni was sure that what she wanted was what God wanted... and she continued to believe, as Donald did, that healing was also part of his will. But after months of praying and trusting – spiritually exhausted – they both began to deal with the possibility that they had, in fact, been mistaken. Donald began to withdraw from Joni – leaving her jealous and confused. But when Steve returned from college on vacation Joni got back to some serious thinking about why it was that God didn't want to heal her.

'Look at this, Joni. Hebrews 11 talks about two categories of people. There are those whose faith was rewarded and those whose faith was not. Some people saw miracles, amazing things. Some didn't. Some had a physical visible reward given from God... some didn't.'

'I hear what you are saying,' Joni admitted. 'And you think I'm part of the group who have not seen their reward?'

'Yes. But I do believe that it is God's will that you be healed. Remember what we talked about before I left... about heaven and what we can look forward to.' Joni nodded. 'You are going to be healed Joni, be certain of it. But God follows his own schedule and it's probably not going to be until you receive your new body in heaven.'

Joni read the scriptures again, prayed with Steve and left it at that. When Donald came back she noticed that something was wrong and before too long she knew what it was.

'I've come to say goodbye,' Donald said as he stood in the doorway of the cottage. 'I never should have kissed you. We should never have allowed this relationship to go on like it has. We talked about marriage and a life together. That was a mistake. I've thought about what I'm doing. There's no turning back. It's over. I'm sorry.'

And with that he was gone leaving Joni weeping in the porchway, calling out his name, begging him to wait.

True Love

Jay came over to look at one of Joni's paintings. Joni had placed the brush down and was reviewing the work from a brief distance. Over the months and years since she had first began to revisit her talent for art – it was amazing to see the progression in her pictures. She was better now than she had been before the accident. It was therapy to take her out of her frustrations and heart-ache and there had been great need of that in her life since Donald had left. Jay squeezed Joni's shoulder and placed her face next to hers.

'Sweet-heart. That's wonderful. We're going to have to hang that one in the sitting room.'

Joni smiled, 'Dad's just asked me to give it to him for the dining room or maybe the kitchen. He hasn't quite made up his mind. So I'm afraid he's beaten you to it.'

'Oh well,' Jay nodded. 'He'll be wanting to show it off to all his friends, "My daughter the brilliant artist," and so you are. I'm proud of you not just for this but for how you've coped, come through the whole Donald thing. It must have been tough.'

Joni sighed. 'It was and I didn't cope that well at first. I was jealous, mean natured. I couldn't stand the fact that others were getting letters from him but I wasn't. But I can see now that it was for the best. We had to put a stop to it... and, though it was painful, Donald's clean break was probably the simplest way. I heard yesterday that he's engaged. He's bringing his fiancée home in a couple of weeks time. I suppose we'll have to meet. It would be strange almost if we didn't. But I know God will help me when the time comes. I just pray he gives me strength and grace.'

Joni picked up the brush again in her mouth and touched up a portion of greenery in the picture. Jay left her to her art and her thoughts.

Joni's thoughts were dwelling on 1 Corinthians 13.

'True love is unselfish, disciplined, directed, self-controlled, patient, kind.'

The brush dropped out of Joni's mouth again as the sobs broke through her throat. 'Oh Lord, I am truly sorry. I know that I've been reading your word and making it mean what I want it to mean instead of waiting for you to show me. I should have realised long ago that you were more than enough for me. Your love, your grace, are all I need.'

Three weeks later God was able to prove to Joni how he was everything she needed. At a Bible study she was introduced to a beautiful young widow, Sandy, Donald's fiancée. And Joni was struck at how beautifully gracious the young woman was, even though she had suffered so much.

Seated next to each other Joni noted how this young woman longed to work for the Lord and serve him with her new husband. Joni was able to turn and smile at Sandy and say, 'I'm so pleased for you and Donald and I want you to know how genuinely happy I am for you both.'

If the year of 1969 had been a good year, 1972 was astounding. Joni saw in herself an amazing change that only God could have done. As she looked towards the end of another year, for the first time she had no human that she could specifically cling to... all she had was God.

'Lord, it's just you and me now. It's taken me a while to get here but I'm here and I know you are faithful. You've proved it to me time and time again. You are the only one I can rely on completely. I know I can trust you and I shall.'

What Now?

Mr and Mrs Eareckson were simply delighted when they finally hung Joni's picture up. 'We'd thought about the dining room and the kitchen but in the end your father liked it so much he insisted that there was only one room where we could hang this picture.'

Joni smiled. 'It looks really good there, Dad. Having it in the office is a good idea. The walls don't look so dull now. It really lifts the place up.'

Mr Eareckson nodded, 'Perfect place to show it off to all my friends who come visiting. Folks is always coming in and out of this office. I might even get you some commissions – get some money coming in for you.'

'Well, it would certainly be good to be a bit more financially independent. But I want my artwork to be accepted on its own merit – not because I'm this poor girl in a wheelchair.'

'What are you talking about, Joni?' her mother exclaimed. 'Those pictures are brilliant!'

'You're supposed to say that,' Joni winked, 'you're my mom.'

'And you're my daughter and wheelchair or no wheelchair, I've always thought you were brilliant. Look at the way you handled that talk on singleness and marriage the other week.'

'But, Mom,' Joni protested, 'I was just telling them like it is. It was just my experience of that particular problem.

I told them about how God has helped me through. It all hinges on that verse that I read in 1 Corinthians, *"Eyes have not seen nor ears heard nor has it entered into the heart of man, the things that God has prepared for those that love him..."*

Joni's mother nodded. 'That's a beautiful scripture, Joni. So full of promise.'

'I just told these girls that when I think about all the things I long for — the ability to walk, to run, to spontaneously reach out and hug someone when I tell them that I love them... I think about that verse and it tells me that God has far better things in store for me in heaven. When I see Diana and her new husband and I wish that somehow that could be me there, loving and being loved, I think about that verse and I realise that what God has in store for me is better than even the tenderest kiss, the sweetest intimacy that I could ever know on this earth. There's nothing here that compares to what lies ahead. The future is the only reality that counts now.'

Joni's Dad came over and kissed Joni on the cheek. 'That's my girl!'

He said the same phrase to a business associate, Mr Millar who was visiting his office the following week. He'd stopped to admire Joni's painting and exclaimed at how original it was. 'I can see that this artist has real style. You have quite an artist here, Eareckson.'

'That's my girl.'

'Your daughter?'

'Yes, her name's Joni. She drew it.'

Standing back a bit further Mr Millar looked at the painting once again. 'It has realistic detail, and shows an unusual discipline.'

Joni's dad was bristling with pride. 'There's one thing you should know,' he added. 'Joni's paralysed. She does all these paintings with her mouth!'

'Incredible! We've just got to get her into an exhibition. It would be wrong to let a talent like this go unnoticed.'

And with that Joni was informed about Mr Millar's plans to arrange a small exhibition in town… just a few paintings and a few contacts to set the ball rolling.

Joni's dad seemed really pleased. 'Millar's got some really good contacts in the business community. You might sell some pictures… make a little money. Who knows what this might start?'

Who knew indeed!

The day for the exhibition arrived and Joni's sisters drove her down town to the Town and Country restaurant where the exhibition was being held.

'Traffic's busy today,' Kathy noted.

'Yes – because look – they've only just gone and closed off that road there. Blocked it completely. Now why would they do that? Are there road works there or something?' Joni asked.

'Not that I can see,' Jay peered round the bollards, negotiating the traffic and trying to work out an alternative route to the exhibition. 'Look here, we'll take this side street. If I can just get round this policeman directing traffic… and the big brass band… and the crowd? What is going on here? What are these people doing? Is there some sort of parade?'

'There must be – but we can't stop and watch, Jay. We've got to get to the exhibition. They'll be expecting us,' Joni urged. 'If you turn this corner we'll be there… yes… just here… and does that banner say what I think it says?' Joni's voice squeeled as her sister's all gasped. A huge banner

spanned the doorway to the Town and Country building:
"Joni Eareckson Day!"

'I can't believe it. What have they done? It's all Millar's fault I know it. He's sprung this. Quick. Hide – in that side street.'

Jay reversed the car at speed round the corner where the girls stared and stared at the scene opening up before their eyes.

'Here comes the brass band!' Linda exclaimed. 'Listen to them play... and is that... no... it can't be? It is! Joni – there's a television crew there. You're going to be on the T.V.'

'There's no getting away from this, Joni. You're going to have to go through with it.' Jay turned to look at her sister with a sympathetic smile.

Joni bit her lip and then agreed. 'Right then. Let's do it.'

Putting the car in gear Jay eased back out onto the street and drove right up to the door of the restaurant. Soon crowds of people and media besieged the car. Carefully Joni was lifted out and people told respectfully to step back. Joni, nervous, felt a lump in her throat. She so desperately wanted these people to look at her art and not at her. But as the day went on she needn't have worried for that was what everyone was here to see.

The media kept the questions to her work. People asked about her inspiration, if she had studied art professionally, if she had any tips or advice, how long it took her to complete a work. The questions came thick and fast and Joni was overwhelmed by the interest and the numbers of people attending.

Joni was fascinated to hear, during the course of the day, that she had earned almost $1000 from her paintings. She had never dreamed that she would earn anything like this from her first show.

And it was an extra special joy to be able to explain to so many people the meaning behind the P.T.L. initials at the bottom of her paintings. On more than one occasion her mind went back to the conversation she had had with Steve Estes that day on the ranch.

'Your paralysis could even be a blessing.'

Joni believed this as yet another person asked her how it was that she could praise God in her situation and did her art express this hope that she found in God. The conversations were varied and exciting and many gave Joni the opportunity to share what God had done in her life.

Then at one point during the ceremonies the crowds thinned a little and Mr Millar walked over to speak to her. Grinning she looked up at him – 'This is all your doing! Small exhibition you said! Huh!'

He laughed. 'There's someone I'd like you to meet.'

Beside him stood a young man, good looking but nervous and awkward. Joni smiled at him, as Mr Millar walked away, and she suggested that he should sit down beside her at the table. He grudgingly agreed and with his hands firmly stuffed in his pockets he sunk into a chair.

Joni tried to start the conversation, 'What do you do?' she asked.

'Nothing.'

Joni thought that this was going to be a very painful drawn out conversation, until the young man opened up a bit more and added, 'I used to be a fireman but I can't work now.'

'Oh? Do you want to tell me about it?' Joni asked. 'Was it in an accident?'

'Yes,' he replied gruffly. His beautiful blue eyes — darkened with bitterness and pain. Easing his hands out from his pockets he held up two scarred stumps where once had been healthy working hands. 'Look — I burnt my hands so badly I lost them. I'd have committed suicide if only I could have used my arms to do it. Right now I don't know what to do. I just can't cope.' The last sentence exploded out of him full of anger and frustration pent up for so long. 'Look at these ugly stumps!'

Joni breathed calmly and began… 'Mr Millar was right. I think I can help you… You see it happened like this…I still remember the date… 30th July 1967 was like any other day in Maryland… I was planning a beach party with my friends. My new costume was waiting in the wardrobe upstairs and I was phoning round anyone I could think of who would want to come…'

***

'So what did the young man say?' Jay asked as they drove home from the exhibition later that day.

'Well I told him about how a relationship with Jesus Christ gives us access to God and all his power. I shared how God had been working in my life. I knew I had to share the good news of Jesus Christ with him. It must have been an hour or more that we talked there by that table. I don't know if anything's happened but he went away with a smile on his face… he said he was going to try again.'

'Well that's something, Joni! I'd say you got through to that young man. You know… you never would have been able to do what you did just there if you hadn't been in a wheelchair.'

Joni looked out the window at the streaming traffic, the street lights, the distant buildings and mass of humanity. Not for the first time that evening Joni had come across the realisation that her paralysis was a blessing – to her and to others.

'I have found a way to serve you, Lord! All these questions and prayers that I've been asking throughout the years – so often I accused you of not answering or not listening at all. I should have known that you knew what you were doing! From the standpoint of eternity my body is just a flicker in the timespan of forever. But there are eternal souls out there who need you – broken hearts in need of your healing. You have people you want me to reach, to touch, with this message of hope. I am here to serve you Lord. Send me where you will.'

God's Choices – Your Changes

Jenny closed the book with a sigh. She'd pass it on to Garry and James tomorrow to let them finish the final chapters. The whole book had been a huge learning experience for her. Looking at the cover she saw the picture of the young woman on the wheelchair – a pounding ocean in the background. The whole thing had made Jenny think about lots of things, about her life, the choices she'd been making – and not just connected with school.

'Looking on that Joni and Friends website was amazing. When she spoke to that young fireman at the exhibition it was only the start. Now she is reaching out to thousands of other people with disabilities. And she is not the only one. Hundreds of other people have joined her. When you think about what that one conversation started – it's staggering. And then to let people make a film about your life!

'Before I read this book I'd have done anything to have film crews and cameras record *The Life of Jenny* with me in the starring role. Now I'm not so sure. If I'm honest I wouldn't want to record the real thing – just some edited highlights. That's what this book has taught me if anything. I'm not what I should be… I've been slacking with my Bible reading; the decisions I make are what I want – God doesn't come into it at all. And then when I want to soothe my conscience I turn it all around to make it sound as if it's what God wanted all along.'

Jenny flicked on the website once again to look at the links and summaries of what had been happening in Joni's life since that day in 1967 when she had jumped into Chesapeake Bay and broken her neck. Jenny read more thoroughly about how her church could make sure that children with special needs and disabilities felt included and part of things. She read about training days and found links to other websites where people in her area were doing things for disabled people. 'She's even met the American president,' Jenny gasped as she scanned down one of the web pages. 'Mrs Tada's role as a disability advocate led to a presidential appointment to the National Council on Disability for three and a half years, during which time the Americans with Disabilities Act became law.'

'She's spoken to millions on TV chat shows in the states and the U.K. She even got married in the end to a man called Ken Tada. So God did have someone planned for her all along. Only she knew that she had to leave these things with God and she did.'

Curious Jenny flicked through some more web pages. Joni's romance with Ken, whom she'd met at church, was an exciting example of how God was in control. Joni had been content to remain single. She'd thought it was part of God's better plan... but in the end he surprised her and her life changed again. In 1982, on a warm summer's day, it had been Joni's turn to wear the white dress and go down the aisle – her wheelchair decked out in ribbons and her proud father gave her away. Ken, a school teacher, was perfect for Joni. They were a great team. Jenny could see that by photos of the two of them meeting the president, of Ken helping Joni with their *Wheels for the World* campaign. Jenny smiled as she read about how they both coped with marriage and how Ken really enjoyed Joni's cooking.

Jenny looked at the Bible on the bedside table – the

dust on the cover told her exactly what it had told Joni all these years ago. Jenny didn't want to think about how long it had been since she had spent some one on one time with God. It was too long. This year had been so full of exams and decisions, stress and hard work... she had barely stopped for God. Any free time was spent with her friends, Garry and James, who were usually a good influence... though not always... Jenny had other friends who had been enticing her away from what she knew was right.

'What was it that Joni learned she had to do about sin?' Jenny wrinkled her brow as she tried to remember something she'd read or heard. 'That's right — "flee from sin don't flirt with it." I've got things all wrong here,' Jenny sighed. 'I just hope that God's going to have time for me. I haven't had time for him these last few months.' And then another line sprang into Jenny's mind. 'I think it might be from the Bible,' Jenny pondered as she tried to get just the right phrase, 'Yes — this is it — "God does not deal with us according to our sins and our iniquities." It is from the Bible, I remember now. She realised that God doesn't treat us as we deserve and that if we trust in Christ then our sin and punishment was dealt with by him at Calvary.'

Jenny stretched herself as she got up off the chair and moved towards the window. The sound of a couple of whizzing cycles coming up the road with two out of tune voices singing along to some discordant pop song told her that Garry and James were on their way.

Putting the book down Jenny bowed her head. They would have to wait — she had an appointment to keep with God. 'And I've got some serious changes to make... I know I'm a sinner and that I need help. I have a life to live and choices to make and I'm not doing this on my own!'

Joni Eareckson Tada: Life Summary

Born in 1949 to John and Margaret Eareckson. Joni Eareckson was married to Ken Tada on July 3rd 1982.

A student at Woodlawn High School, Maryland, Baltimore, a diving accident in 1967 left her a quadriplegic in a wheelchair, unable to use her hands. During two years of rehabilitation, she spent long months learning how to paint with a brush between her teeth. Today her high detail, fine art, paintings and prints are highly collectable and sought after.

Due to her best-selling books, beginning with her autobiography, Joni has visited 35 countries. Her first name is recognized around the world. World Wide Pictures' full-length feature film, JONI, in which she recreated her own life, has been translated into 15 languages and shown in scores of countries around the world.

Joni's role as a disability advocate led to a presidential appointment to the National Council on Disability for three and a half years, during which time the Americans with Disabilities Act became law.

Joni and Friends was founded in 1979 and has grown into four flagship programs that affect the lives of thousands of disabled people and their families. In 2002, Joni and Friends served almost 500 special needs families through twelve Family Retreats across the U.S.A. Through *Wheels for the World*, over 24,000 wheelchairs have been collected nationwide since 1994, refurbished and shipped to developing nations where physical therapists fit each chair to a needy disabled child or adult. Joni and Friends, a daily five minute radio program, is heard over 850 broadcast outlets and has received the "Radio Program of the Year" award from National Religious Broadcasters. Through ten Area Ministries offices, Joni and Friends teams provide church training and education to promote inclusion of people with disabilities.

A highly sought-after conference speaker both in the U.S. and internationally Joni is also a columnist for the United Kingdom's

Christian Herald, and several European Christian magazines. She also serves on several boards, including the Lausanne Committee for World Evangelization as Senior Associate on Disability Concerns and the Board of Reference for the Christian Medical and Dental Society.

Joni Eareckson Tada has received The American Academy of Achievement's Golden Plate Award; The Courage Award from the Courage Rehabilitation Center; The Award of Excellence from the Patricia Neal Rehabilitation Center; The Victory Award from the National Rehabilitation Hospital; The Golden Word Award from the International Bible Society. She is also currently the Honorary Co-Chair of the United States Presidential Prayer Team. In 2003 the Evangelical Christian Press Association presented Joni with their Lifetime Achievement Award.

You can read these books for further information on the life of Joni Eareckson: Joni: - 25th Anniversary Edition by Joni Eareckson Tada; The God I Love by Joni Eareckson Tada.

If you want to contact Joni and Friends:

US Postal Address:
Headquarters Joni and Friends,
PO Box 3333, Agoura Hills, CA 91376-3333
Phone (U.S.A.) 818 -707-5664 Fax (U.S.A.) 818-707-2391
website: www.joniandfriends.org
UK contact details:
PO Box 353, Epsom, Surrey, KT18 5WS
Phone : 01372 749955   Fax: 01372 737040
www.throughtheroof.org
email: info@throughtheroof.org
Northern Ireland details:
Joni and Friends
PO Box 143, BANGOR
County Down, BT19 6BY N I
Phone: 028 9145 0681

Joni Eareckson Time Line

(from before her birth to present day)

1945: End of World War II.

1949: Joni Eareckson born, October 15th 1949.

1950: Credit card invented.

1952: Princess Elizabeth crowned Queen in the U.K. aged 25.

1953: DNA discovered.
Sweet rationing ends in the United Kingdom.

1954: Bannister breaks 4 minute mile.

1957: Dr Suess publishes *The Cat in the Hat*.

1961: Berlin wall built.
Soviet Union launches first man in space.
John F Kennedy sworn in as president.

1962: Cuban misile crisis.

1963: John F Kennedy assasinated.
Martin Luther King's *I have a dream,* speech.

1964: *The Beatles* launched in the United States.
Joni Eareckson accepts Jesus Christ.

1965: Vietnam war.
Winston Churchill dies.

1967: Joni Eareckson's diving accident.
First heart transplant.

1968: Martin Luther King assassinated.

1969: First man on the moon.
Joni leaves hospital/rehab.

1970: Computer floppy disks invented.

1971: Women in Switzerland get the vote.

1973: United States pulls out of Vietnam.
Picasso dies.

1974: Joni appears on *The Today Show*.
1976: Joni's first book published.
1979: Joni and Friends founded and the movie is launched.
1980: Alfred Hithcock dies.
Olympic Games held in Moscow.
1982: Joni Eareckson gets married and becomes Joni Eareckson Tada, July 3rd 1982.
Joni's radio ministry begins.
1985: Famine in Ethiopia.
Wreck of the Titanic found.
1986: Space shuttle Challenger explodes.
1989: Berlin Wall falls.
Tian'anmen Square Massacre in China.
1990: Hubble Telescope launched into space.
Americans with Disabilities Act becomes law.
1991: Collapse of the Soviet Union.
South Africa repeals Apartheid laws.
1997 Joni awarded silver medal in the C.S. Lewis awards.
1998: Titanic becomes most successful movie ever.
2000: Year of the Millennium.
2001: Twin towers attack, September 11th 2001.
More than 3 milion copies of *Joni* are in print.
2002: *Wheels for the World* donates over 24,000 wheelchairs to over 50 countries since 1994.
April 10th, Joni meets U.S. President George W. Bush.
2003: Joni Eareckson Tada receives Life Time Achievement Award from The Evangelical Christian Press Association.

Thinking Further: Chapter 1
Life Choices?

The three friends had to make some important decisions and they didn't quite know how to go about them. Who do you ask for help when trying to make a big decision? In Psalm 32: 8, God promises to watch over and guide those who trust in him. The decisions they made all depended on hopes and plans they had for the future. What would you like to do in the future? How do you think you would feel if something happened that meant that you couldn't do any of these things?

Dear God,
Please help me to turn to you for your guidance and to turn to your word for help and advice. Please help me in my life when difficult things happen or when people judge me because of my looks or abilities. Help me not to feel bitter and angry but to treat them in the same way that Jesus treated those who mocked and judged him. You showed mercy and love even to your enemies Jesus. Help me to be more like you.

Please help churches and organisations that support people with disabilities and empower them to do their best. Help my church and youth group to be welcoming to people and kids with special needs.
Amen.

Thinking Further: Chapter 2
That Day on the Beach

When Joni began to realise what had happened to her, all of the everyday things that had distracted her and even kept her from thinking about God were chased from her mind. What kind of things do you think about the most? Do these things really matter the way that knowing God matters? Joshua 1: 8 records God's command to Joshua to think about God's word day and night so that he would be careful to obey it. How often do you read and think about the Bible?

Dear God,
Please help me to concentrate daily on you and on what you say to me in the Bible. Sometimes I can choose to do other things instead of reading your word or talking to you. Please change my heart so that I long to make you the most important person in my life.

Please help those organisations that are reaching out to people with disabilities to give them your word and teach them about you. Please help charities who produce material for the blind so that they too can read your word through brail or hear it on audio cassettes or CD's. Thank you for giving me your word so that I can listen to it or read it for myself.
Amen.

Thinking Further: Chapter 3
White Coats and Green Pastures

Where did the words that Joni's father taught her come from? (The number 23 is a bit of a hint.) Who is it that promises to be with us through even the most difficult times? Joni's prayer showed that she wasn't sure that God was with her. Does that mean that he wasn't? How does God manage to be in and with us all the time? (see John 14: 15-21)

Dear God,
Thank you for being with me always as you have promised. Remind me when I am afraid to turn to you for comfort. Help me to give comfort to those who need encouragement, love and friendship.

Please be with people who are working in the community as companions to those who are lonely or house bound. Give them wisdom, courage and safety.
Amen.

Thinking Further: Chapter 4
Before it all Began

What did the camp leader use to show God's perfect standard? How did Joni feel when she realised how good God was? She trusted in Jesus to live up to the standard for her. Do you think that Jesus is willing to save anyone who trusts in him the way that he saved Joni? (John 3:16 and Hebrews 13:8) Who was Joni more grateful for finding: God or Jason?

Dear God,
Thank you for your love and forgiveness. Teach me from your word the reality of your love. Show me how much I need you and how wonderful you are.
    Please encourage and help those people who are working with missions to disabled people around the world. Help those organisations that are struggling for funds and support. Thank you for organisations like Joni and Friends that give much needed financial and practical support to Christian charities like these. Provide for their needs and encourage them with wonderful examples of how you can work in the lives of the people they work with.
    Amen.

Thinking Further: Chapter 5
When Life is Like a Punchbag

Joni found that her relationship with Jason was making it difficult for her to keep God's law and to keep herself pure. What sort of things do you find that make it difficult to obey God? What do you think that Jesus would have to say about them? Joni had everything that a girl her age could want but she was not satisfied. Why was this? What do you think she was missing?

Dear God,
Thank you for the wonderful generous gifts that you have given me. Thank you for food and drink, for clothes and for all the extras that I have. So many children and young people around the world do not have the things that I have. Thank you for education, for books, for the ability to read. Thank you for the love and support of family and friends.

Help me to be watchful for people who need my love and support. Help me to be like you and to comfort and befriend the needy. You weren't just friendly with the rich, wealthy and talented people. You showed love to people who no one else was friends with. Thank you for those people in government who are supporting disabled people and those with special needs. Show me how I can do this too in my own life, church and community.
Amen.

Thinking Further: Chapter 6
I'm Walking out of Here!

Joni was determined that she would recover, even in defiance of medical opinion. Does God always heal people when they ask him to? What does he do instead in some cases? (James 1:1-8 and 2 Corinthians 12:7-10) Dick was very faithful to Joni, coming back to visit her every week. How can we understand God's promise never to leave us or forsake us (Hebrews 13:5) in situations where Christians do suffer terribly?

Dear God,
Thank you that you always answer prayer. Help me to realise that you are always listening. Help me to be patient and to accept whatever answer you give me — even if it is no or wait. Sometimes, God, I don't know what answer you are giving me — but help me to be confident in you and that you always know what you are doing.

Thank you for the people who have been faithful to me in my life — thank you, Jesus, for your faithfulness. I can always rely on you whatever happens.

Please help people who are struggling with pain and disability today. May they get in contact with those who will give them help and introduce them to you and your love.
Amen.

Thinking Further: Chapter 7
Physical Therapy

What do you think would frustrate you the most if you were in a situation, like Joni's, where you couldn't even wipe your own nose? Joni's hopes were very high for the prayer meeting that they had for her in the church. How do you think she felt when she woke the next day and found that she was still paralysed? It can be very disappointing and discouraging to have our hopes dashed like that. What can we learn from David's attitude to unanswered prayer in 2 Samuel 12:15-23?

Dear God,
Sometimes I am disappointed and this can be hard to cope with. You know what it is like to be disappointed — especially when your friends left you alone to face your enemies and one even betrayed you. Thank you that I can rely on you and that in the middle of hard times you are with me.

Thank you God for the skills of nurses, doctors and physical therapists who work so hard. Please help those professionals who are working in hospitals and rehabilitation centres and help their patients as they hope for recovery or learn to cope with a new life and new problems.

Amen.

Thinking Further: Chapter 8
Mistletoe and Memories

Not everyone in Joni's ward was a Christian and some, like Jim, posed questions that unsettled and confused her. How should we react to those who doubt and plant doubts in our minds too? How did Joni find reassurance to bring her out of her doubt and depression? Where can we go to find that same reassurance?

What did the decision to start painting and writing say about her changing attitude to her situation? How do you think the words that Joni remembered from Isaiah 26:3 and 55:8 helped her?

Dear God,
Please protect me from untruths and lies that are sometimes taught in schools and in books. Help me to remember that your word is true. When I read something help me to remember your word and to work out whether these words are against you or for you. When I read books that tell lies, help me to be able to tell others how I know that this stuff is wrong. Give me the right words to say.

Please help nurses and therapists who are working with people with depression. Be with those Christians who are working in situations like this. Help them to give the right help and to be able to share something about you and your peace. Thank you that you do give peace to those whose mind rests on you.
Amen.

Thinking Further: Chapter 9
Praise The Lord

Joni was bitterly disappointed when all her high hopes of using her hands again were dashed. She began to feel angry with God and rebel against him in her thoughts. What did Jesus say about sinning in our thoughts? (Matthew 5:21-30) Do you sin against God in your thoughts? What can you do about this? How should we react to disappointment and seeing our hopes dashed? Read Habbakuk 3:17-19, do you think that it is easy to react in this way?

Dear God,
I am sorry for my sin. Show me how I can please you more. Help me to focus my thoughts on you and to keep them pure.

Please be with the families and friends of people who are suffering from illness, depression and physical injuries. Help them as they struggle with the shock and heartache and help them when their friend or family member comes home. May they have the strength and wisdom to know what to do and how to help.
Amen.

Thinking Further: Chapter 10
The Summer of '69

Steve helped Joni to realise that God's purpose for her injury might be to help others rather than to punish her. Read John 9: 1-7 and think about God's purposes being fulfilled through difficulty. Meeting with others to study God's word helped Joni to understand her situation. Does the Bible give us any promises about the help that we can get from other Christians? (Proverbs 27:17, Matthew 18:20 and Hebrews 10:24 and 25 might be good places to look.)

Dear God,
Thank you for the people who have taught me about you. Thank you for family, Sunday school teachers and pastors who have taught me from your word. Help me to learn more about you so that I can teach others and gain wisdom. Thank you that your message is not complicated and that even the smallest child can learn that Jesus loves them.

Thank you for the organisation that Joni Eareckson set up: Joni and Friends. Thank you that they are reaching out to help those with special needs and disabilities and that they teach so many people about you. Thank you for how you have used Joni's life to bring glory to you.
Amen.

Thinking Further: Chapter 11
True Love

1 Corinthians 13 is one of the best-known passages in scripture and it tells us about love. Read it and think about where we find that love shown most clearly (see John 15: 13). How do we know that God loves us and that we can rely on him when all others fail? It can be very easy to trust other people or their skills and abilities, it can even be easy to trust in ourselves. How did Joni's experiences help her to understand this and to place all her hope and trust in God?

Dear God,
Thank you for your love and that you are love. Help me to show your love to everyone I know. Please help me to show love and patience and kindness to the people that I am with in my family and to my friends. Sometimes it is easy to be on my best behaviour with some and then rude to others who I know won't criticize me for it. Make me thankful for patient and loving friends and family. May I not take them for granted.

Thank you for the lives of so many disabled people who are hard working, talented, disciplined followers of you. Thank you for their witness and their prayers and the wonderful work that they do for you. Help me to learn from their lives and from the life of Joni.
Amen.

Thinking Further: Chapter 12
What Now?

What kind of plans would Joni have had when she realised that she would never have the use of her hands? Do you think that they would have included an art exhibition? Her testimony was a great help to the young man who had lost his hands. Why was she able to speak to him in a way that no one else could?

As Joni looked out of the window, she felt pity for the many broken hearts that she saw in the world. Can you think of times when Jesus expressed similar pity for lost people? (Try looking in Matthew 9: 37 & 38 and Luke 13: 31-35.)

Dear God,
Help me to use my gifts to glorify you. Show me what you want me to do. Sometimes I might think I am not good at anything. Sometimes I might think that you can't use the things that I am good at. But help me to remember that whatever I do — I should do it for you and that I should do it as well as I can… even if that is a football game, homework, cleaning the dishes, smiling, singing, and being loving and generous.

Thank you, God, for how you give us gifts of creativity. Thank you, God, for the gifts of love that you give to people who help and comfort others who are suffering. This is a gift that you give to people who are disabled too. Thank you that you can use the problems and difficulties in our lives to bless others and glorify you.
Amen.

Thinking Further: Chapter 13
God's Choices — Your Changes

If your life were to be made into a film, how much of it would you want to have edited out? Who is it that guides and controls your decisions? Joni's life reminded Jenny that God does not deal with us according to our sins and iniquities (Psalm 103:10). Have you put your trust in Jesus so that you can be sure that your sin has been dealt with on the cross?

Dear God,
Thank you that you have not dealt with me in the way that I deserve but that you have shown great mercy. You have already given me so much in my life — your generosity and love is like nothing I have ever known or will know.

Please be with the people who work alongside Joni at Joni and Friends as they meet with people in positions of authority and with people in churches who want to know how to help the disabled and with people who are struggling with the problems of disability itself. Give them wisdom and strength, the right words to say and the support that they need to do the job that you want them to do.

Amen.

Answers

Chapter 2: * Nothing matters more than knowing God * Read Mattehw 16:26 - There is nothing more valuable than your soul. **Chapter 3**: *Psalm 23 *The Lord God *God is with us always - Matthew 28:20 *Through the Holy Spirit. **Chapter 4:** *The Ten Commandments *She felt that she was a sinner and couldn't save herself *Yes - God loved the world that he sent his son so that whosoever believes in him should not perish. *God. **Chapter 5:** *She was missing the peace of God. **Chapter 6:** *No he doesn't *Perseverance; maturity; completeness; wisdom. *When we are weak we are strong in God's strength. It stops us from being conceited. He comforts us in troubles and brings us through them not necessarily out of them. **Chapter 7:** *We learn that we should accept God's answer and realise that it is for the best. We shouldn't rebel and be angry but accept that God knows what he is doing. **Chapter 8:** *Joni found assurance in God's word. *We can too. *She was accepting it and God's will. *They showed her where and how to get peace. It helped her to deal with her doubts and confusion as she realised that God did things differently and that he understands and knows everything. **Chapter 9:** *Sinful thoughts and emotions are just as wrong as sinful actions. *We should rejoice and be joyful in God our Saviour. **Chapter 10:** *The man was blind but Jesus used his problem to show the world God's power. Though Joni wasn't healed God has also used her disability to show the world his power in her life. *Christians inspire each other; Jesus is with them; Christians encourage each other. **Chapter 11:** *Jesus Christ. *He sent his son to die for us on the cross. Jesus went through so much for us. *Because of the accident Joni couldn't rely on herself to do things - other people couldn't always be there either - only God. **Chapter 12:** *She couldn't use her hands either. *Jesus cried over Jerusalem and he longed for people to work for God to save souls. **Chapter 13:** *God.

LIGHTKEEPERS
Real lives! Real Adventures!

Ten boys who changed the world
David Livingstone, Billy Graham, Brother Andrew,
John Newton, William Carey, George Müller, Nicky
Cruz, Eric Liddell, Luis Palau, Adoniram Judson.
1-85792-5793

Ten boys who made a difference
Augustine of Hippo, Jan Hus, Martin Luther, Ulrich
Zwingli, William Tyndale, Hugh Latimer, John Calvin,
John Knox, Lord Shaftesbury, Thomas Chalmers.
1-85792-7753

Ten boys who made history
C H Spurgeon, Jonathan Edwards, Samuel
Rutherford, D L Moody, Martin Lloyd Jones, A W
Tozer, John Owen, Robert Murray McCheyne, Billy
Sunday, George Whitfield.
1-85792-8369

Ten girls who changed the world
Corrie Ten Boom, Mary Slessor, Joni Eareckson
Tada, Isobel Kuhn, Amy Carmichael,
Elizabeth Fry, Evelyn Brand, Gladys Aylward,
Catherine Booth, Jackie Pullinger
1-85792-6498

Ten girls who made a difference
Monica of Thagaste, Catherine Luther, Susanna
Wesley, Ann Judson, Maria Taylor, Susannah
Spurgeon, Bethan Lloyd-Jones, Edith Schaeffer,
Sabina Wurmbrand, Ruth Bell Graham.
1-85792-7761

Ten girls who made history
Ida Scudder, Betty Green, Jeanette Li,
Mary Jane Kinnaird, Bessie Adams, Emma Dryer,
Lottie Moon, Florence Nightingale,
Heanrietta Mears, Elisabeth Elliot.
1-85792-8377

Trailblazers

Staying faithful - Reaching out!

Christian Focus Publications publishes books for adults and children under its three main imprints: Christian Focus, Mentor and Christian Heritage. Our books reflect that God's word is reliable and Jesus is the way to know him, and live for ever with him.

Our children's publication list includes a Sunday school curriculum that covers pre-school to early teens; puzzle and activity books. We also publish personal and family devotional titles, biographies and inspirational stories that children will love.

If you are looking for quality Bible teaching for children then we have an excellent range of Bible story and age specific theological books.

From pre-school to teenage fiction, we have it covered!

Find us at our web page:
www.christianfocus.com